PLUM ISLAND

To Mark

Dyke C. Henduckson

PLUM ISLAND

A VULNERABLE GEM

DYKE HENDRICKSON

AMERICA
THROUGH TIME®
ADDING COLOR TO AMERICAN HISTORY

America Through Time is an imprint of Fonthill Media LLC
www.through-time.com
office@through-time.com

Published by Arcadia Publishing by arrangement with Fonthill Media LLC
For all general information, please contact Arcadia Publishing:
Telephone: 843-853-2070
Fax: 843-853-0044
E-mail: sales@arcadiapublishing.com
For customer service and orders:
Toll-Free 1-888-313-2665

www.arcadiapublishing.com

First published 2022

ISBN 978-1-63499-401-9

Typeset in 10pt on 13pt Sabon
Printed and bound in England

Foreword

The names of hundreds of visitors to Plum Island have been carved into the walkway leading from the Wildlife Refuge's Lot 1 to the ocean. All planks have been inscribed. More names could likely be affixed if the walkway were longer because Plum Island—and the Parker River National Wildlife Refuge—is a natural resource that many people love.

Plum Island is an 11-mile-long barrier island off Newburyport, Massachusetts. Both ends of the island face challenges. On the northern sector, some houses are vulnerable to rising seas. In the southern portion, scientists are concerned that climate change will affect the health and travel habits of migrating birds.

There are challenges aplenty to this remarkable resource.

This book is about the history and the changing conditions at the island. Plum Island is not exactly at a crucial crossroads because records and photos suggest that it has existed through many significant transitions. However, residential build-up is affecting the northern section, and climate change is raising issues for the southern portion. In 2022, the island is immersed in a significant moment of its history.

Some oceanside homes at the northern point of the island are using sandbags to keep the tides from coming over the disappearing dunes. A visitor from another universe might find this strange. Sandbags holding back an ocean? Yet that is one of the stopgaps used to halt erosion at Reservation Terrace. Further south, also on the inhabited section of the barrier island, wealthy homeowners have been bringing in boulders to keep the ocean back and the dunes in place. It seems to be working, but this practice is converting parts of a sand beach into a rock-strewn landscape.

Those not familiar with the area might ask why so many houses are built on this barrier island. Indeed, some handsome residences in recent years have been constructed on the exact parcels of land where cottages had stood before falling into the ocean. One answer is that the ocean views are so spectacular and the island ambience so appealing that they are willing to take the risks.

A late friend of mine, business owner and civic leader Josiah Welch, lived in an oceanside home on 49th Street.

Plum Island, on the north shore of Massachusetts, is a complex combination of marsh, beach, dunes, wildlife refuge, and residential development. (*Steve Atherton Collection*)

Numerous walkways enable visitors to enjoy the island's beauty. (*Dan Graovac photo*)

The view was breathtaking, regardless of the weather. Similarly, P.I. activist Bob Connors owns an oceanside home on Annapolis Way in Newbury. He is so close to the eroding beach that he has driven down long steel pilings to keep his house from falling off the lip of the property. Yet he stays.

This book touches on aspects of Plum Island's past as well as the present. It references several important events of island history, including a donation in 1929 by philanthropist Annie H. Brown so land could be purchased for what is now the Parker River National Wildlife Refuge. It also explains a political war of words in the 1940s that pitted birdwatchers against bird hunters. In addition, the chapters illustrate how homeowners in recent years have fortified the beaches with boulders, so their houses are not devastated by erosion.

This presentation does not offer often-seen old news photos that pictured storm-wracked houses falling into the Atlantic. That story has been told. This tome attempts to highlight natural beauty and amazing wildlife that are part of the "modern" Plum Island.

One takeaway for readers is this: Plum Island is spectacular, and it will go on.

Acknowledgments

I want to thank the Bowlen Charitable Trust, managed by Newburyport attorney James Connolly, for extending grants so this book could be written. The Bowlen Trust has supported my Merrimack trilogy: *Merrimack: The Resilient River* (2021); *New England Coast Guard Stories: Remarkable Mariners* (2020); and *Nautical Newburyport: A History of Captains, Clipper Ships and the Coast Guard* (2017).

Plum Island: A Vulnerable Gem is my fourth local maritime book. I am currently devising a plan that will enable me to give books away at schools, clubs, and reading groups. One of my goals is to inform young people what is happening in their (local) natural world.

I would also like to thank photographers Dan Graovac, Steve Atherton, and Bryan Eaton for contributing excellent photos. Dan took terrific shots of birds, coastlines, and even a feeding whale. Steve contributed fine aerial shots that few have seen. Bryan, for many years a valued photographer for *The Daily News*, provided images that depict numerous facets of the island

Also, I want to thank Newburyport librarian Sharon Spieldenner for helping me with computer issues, and John Macone and Matt Thorne of the Merrimack River Watershed Council for their support. If an image does not have a photo credit, it was likely taken by me—Dyke Hendrickson.

Contents

Foreword   5

Acknowledgments   9

  1   Early Days of Plum Island: Native-Americans Gave Way to Europeans   13

  2   Early Days of Plum Island Marked by Fun, Tragedy   17

  3   Early Hotels Fostered a Vibrant Social Life on the Beach   24

  4   Popularity, Density of Plum Island Has Increased in Past Two Decades   33

  5   Two Civilizations Exist on One Barrier Island   38

  6   Plum Island North: Efforts Increase to Halt Erosion   47

  7   Last "Old Hotel" to Be Torn Down   50

  8   Sand "Mining" Eyed as Plum Island Remedy   52

  9   An Outsider Looks at the Challenges on Plum Island   54

 10   Two Civilizations Share One Barrier Island   61

 11   The History of the Parker River National Wildlife Refuge   64

 12   Through the Years: A History of the Audubon Society   72

 13   The U.S. Fish and Wildlife Service Has Been a Leader on Plum Island   75

 14   Rachel Carson, Environmentalist and Promoter of Plum Island   78

 15   Parker River: A National Wildlife Refuge   82

 16   Federal Duck Stamp Has Helped Wildlife   94

 17   Naturalist Mark Garland Offers Advice on Birdwatching   98

18 Plum Island Took Bronze for "Hottest" Birding Site   99

19 The Preservation of the Popular Piping Plover   101

20 Osprey: Spring Signals Return of a Bird That Can Really Fish   103

21 Audubon Leaders Express Concern about Effect of
      Climate Change on Coastal Birds   106

22 Plum Island Airport Has a Long and Colorful History   109

23 A Rumrunning Boat, a Foggy Plum Island Evening and
      a Coast Guardsman Is Killed During Prohibition   112

24 A Cleaner Merrimack River Will Help Plum Island   118

Bibliography   121
About the Author   123

1

Early Days of Plum Island:
Native-Americans Gave Way to Europeans

Excerpts here are from the work of the late Nancy Weare, in her book *Plum Island: The Way it Was*, published in 1993. This portion comes from documents managed by Historical Ipswich, an organization and website dedicated to North Shore history. Permission to use her work was granted by Gordon Harrison, Ipswich town historian and a friend of the family.

The narrow barrier island of sand dune and marsh that we recognize today as Plum Island is believed to have started as a sandspit perhaps as many as 6,000 years ago. As it increased in area, its southern end eventually attached itself to four glacial-drumlin islands that are today called Cross Farm Hill, Bar I lead, Ipswich Bluffs and Grape Island. In length, the island extends from its northern extremity at the mouth of the Merrimack River to Bar Head, which rises majestically to overlook the mouth of the Ipswich River.

Plum Island was first recorded on European charts in the early seventeenth century. We surmise that local Indians had found the island an agreeable summer habitation. There is some speculation but no agreement that Vikings had stopped there centuries earlier, and we know that Champlain sailed by the island during his exploration of the Massachusetts coast. Captain John Smith, who visited our shores in 1614, described the island in some detail, although he did not give it a name.

The island was included in the 1621-22 land grant to Captain John Mason when the president and council of Plymouth granted to him, under the name Mariana, "… all the land lying along the Atlantic from Naumkeag River to the Merrimack River … together with the Great Isle or Island henceforth to be called Isle Mason lying near or before the Bay, Harbor or ye river Aggawom." However, the name Plumb Island is the one recorded on local maps, very likely in recognition of its many plum hushes, and is the one that prevailed.

For the first one hundred and fifty years of the nearby settlements of Newbury, Rowley and Ipswich, Plum Island was treated primarily as a resource. In the beginning days of the colony, open pastureland was limited, and the island's marshes, or meadows,

A blustery winter storm hits Plum Island, the southern sector of which is part of the Parker River National Wildlife Refuge. (*Steve Atherton Collection*)

offered grazing for the colonists' livestock. The salt hay was also used for bedding and mulching and as insulation along the foundations of houses. The trees mentioned in the earliest descriptions of the island were probably cut for lumber and floated to the mainland. We are certain that pines existed, since they were used to define the land boundaries in some of the early deeds. Only at the southern end of Plum Island, where the higher ground of the glacial drumlins provided rich topsoil, was there any attempt at settlement.

Plum Island was not included in the territories granted to the early settlers of Ipswich, Rowley and Newbury but was under the jurisdiction of the General Court. In 1639 two residents of Ipswich obtained permission to keep "fourscore hoggs on the island ... from Aprille next until harvest he got in...." The town of Newbury responded by asking for title to the whole island. For the next ten years the three settlements shared the island. Eventually in 1649 the General Court divided Plum Island among the townships, two fifths each being awarded to Ipswich and Newbury and one fifth to Rowley.

Even in colonial times there was concern about erosion, and the selectmen tried through regulations to prevent the destruction of the dunes lest the shifting sands overrun the valuable salt meadows.

In the summer of 1769 Newbury and Newburyport, which had by then become separate towns (1764), joined together to share the cost of a hospital to be built on Plum Island to shelter and care for those who were ill with smallpox. This highly contagious

Sunrise at Plum Island can provide memorable beauty. (*Dan Graovac photo*)

disease was greatly feared, and it was the custom to isolate the afflicted. The hospital, or Pest House, was located near the northern end of the island to make it accessible to ships arriving from foreign ports where seamen were often exposed to both smallpox and yellow fever and needed to be kept in quarantine. If an incoming ship had disease on board, it was required to be washed down with vinegar, and its soft goods, such as cloth, were buried in sand for nine days.

The Pest House was also used to care for residents who had smallpox. Not all the patients were cooperative. Comments taken from a letter sent to a patient by Newburyport's selectmen indicate how seriously these rules were to be observed: "if you should come away before you are Cleansed, the People in Town will Stone you out again." Instructions to staff included the following: "we desire you to be extremely Careful that you Burn nothing in the fires, but to Bury everything that is Offensive to cover it with earth as soon as put in the place for that purpose, and when the Cows shall be put into the Pastures we desire you to keep them away as far as you can from the Fence."

At the time of the Revolution, forts were erected on both sides of the river to guard the harbor entrance. The funding for Plum Island's fort was undertaken jointly by Newbury and Newburyport. The historian Joshua Coffin wrote that Newburyport "voted to allow the soldiers stationed on Plum Island candles and sweetening for their beer." The fort, called Fort Faith, was eventually washed away. During the War of 1812, a temporary fort was built.

As shipping increased along the coast and particularly in the Merrimack, there was a need for range lights to guide incoming ships. In 1783 a group of private citizens provided the funding. These beacons were later replaced with two small wooden lighthouses and a keeper's dwelling.

An ever-growing number of shipwrecks on the shores of Plum Island caused the Newburyport Marine Society in 1787 to build and equip two shelters for the use of shipwrecked sailors in winter storms. Unless a ship was stranded on an offshore bar, the crew were sometimes able to reach shore alive, but without shelter it was likely that they would perish from exposure before their plight was known. A few years later, in 1804, the Merrimack Humane Society added additional huts. The locations of such shelters along our coast were described in leaflets that were carried aboard ships using these waters.

In 1829 an attempt was made to increase the depth of water at the bar at the mouth of the Merrimack by the construction of a breakwater extending from Plum Island to Woodbridge Island. Congress appropriated $32,000 for the purpose, later adding to that sum before the project was completed in 1831. The breakwater did not prove to be effective and eventually was destroyed by wave and water action.

2

Early Days of Plum Island Marked by Fun, Tragedy

This chapter was written by E. Vale Smith in 1854. Euphemia was a historian and a sociologist. Her work appears here because it focuses on an aspect of Plum Island that is sometimes overlooked—loss of life and treasure from shipwrecks. Scores of calamities occurred off Plum Island; hundreds of men died. Though she wrote about many aspects of life in the Newburyport area, her observations about shipwrecks and loss of life are an important part of the Plum Island story. Research at the Custom House Maritime Museum in Newburyport details a staggering number of wrecks from 1772 to 1936. Her book was *History of Newburyport; From the Earliest Settlement of the Country to the Present Time* (published by the author in 1854, printed by Damrell and Moore in Boston).

The mouth of the Merrimack River is narrow. It is shallow, with sandbars frequently forming to make navigation difficult. The brisk current of the river runs east; powerful ocean tides come from the west. Moving up the river to the port of Newburyport was very difficult, especially before the arrival of steam engines. Here are observations of Euphemia Vale Smith, from the book, *History of Newburyport*.

There is no native of Newburyport, and scarcely a stranger who has visited our city in the summer season, who does not retain vivid recollections of this fantastic strip of sand, Plum Island.

To the minds of most, its associations are of the social gatherings of friends, of sea-side picnics with home companions and stranger guests; the eye recalls the sandy beach dotted with tents; the cloth spread on the clean yellow sand, surrounded with groups of young men and maidens, old men and children, the complacent pastor and the grave deacon, all enjoying together a day of unrestrained mirth and healthful recreation, some indulging in the exuberance of their wild delight amid the waves that roll their white crests to the feet of the more timid watchers, and others preparing the gondola for a return home, knocking away the poles that support the tents, or packing up the fragments of the feast preparatory to stowing them in the carriage, wagon or boat, that is waiting to carry people home, just as the sun is setting behind the western hills.

Thousands remember just such scenes as these when they think of Plum Island. But there is another picture, with darker shades, which comes between the eye and heart at the mention of Plum Island. There are some to whom that name recalls a dark, stormy night: the heavy moaning of the sea, a bark vainly striving to clear the breakers, blinding snow, a slippery deck, stiff and glazed ropes, hoarse commands that the cruel winds seize and carry far away from the ear of the sailor, a crash of tons of falling water beating in the hatches, shrieks which no man heard, and ghastly corpses on the deceitful, shifting sands, and the great ocean cemetery, still holding in awful silence the lost bodies of the dead.

When the northeast wind blows, and the misty fog, which has left its home in the Bay of Fundy, and travelled down the coast, shrouding from sight the breakers and the bar, and dimming the warning harbor lights, when the drizzling rain turns to the fierce tempest, and the deep roar of the Atlantic can be heard like mournful dirges in the streets, then the citizens of Newburyport think of Plum Island, and speculate on the probability that a vessel may even then be vainly struggling amid the breakers. If in the daytime, one and another, and here and there a party, put on their thickest coats, and stoutest boots, and speed away to Plum Island, to see the storm in its majesty, and to rescue its victims, if any such there are, that may be reached.

In December 1839, occurred one of these terrible storms. On the 15th, there had been a very high tide, which had overflowed the wharves on the riverside, and covered the eastern end of Plum Island with water, so that for some hours the keeper could not get to the lights, a lake having formed between his dwelling-house and the lighthouses.

The hotel nearer the bridge was also surrounded with water, while sandhills twenty feet high were washed away, and others formed, the eastern shore being reduced by the action of the waves, many rods. On the 24th, there was a recurrence of the storm, and during the night, a brig of some three hundred tons, the vessel *Pocahontas*, struck, and was discovered early in the morning, but in such a situation that nothing could be done for the relief of the wretched men who still clung to the wreck.

Those on board in whom life remained, could see the excited but impotent spectators on the shore, while the latter gazed with useless sympathy upon the stragglers in this terrible conflict of the elements. The surf was such that no boat could possibly live in it, and those in the brig were too distant to throw lines on shore, if the wind had not been enlisted against such a means of deliverance.

The bodies of several of the crew were afterwards found on the beach at some distance from the brig, with the small boat lying near, showing that these had attempted thus to escape, but perished by the very means taken to preserve their lives. These probably left the brig before daylight, and perhaps before she struck. Seven bodies of the crew were recovered, besides the captain and first mate.

One man who was seen before nine in the morning on the bowsprit, retained that critical position until near twelve, when a heavy sea washed away him and his support, and he was lost in full sight of scores of spectators. To make his case the sadder, it was but a few minutes after this catastrophe that the brig was washed upon the beach, so that it was readily boarded from the shore. One man was found lashed to the vessel with life not extinct when first discovered, but so exhausted that he ceased to breathe without being able to make an intelligible sign. The sea had beaten over him so fiercely and continuously, that his clothes were almost entirely washed off him.

On the Beach, Plum Island, Mass.

Tourists have enjoyed the island for more than a century, as this postcard from the late nineteenth century indicates. (*Newburyport Archival Center of the Newburyport Public Library*)

Many shipwrecks have taken place off Plum Island, in part because the harbor entrance is narrow, and the water is shallow. (*Newburyport Archival Center of the Newburyport Public Library*)

Still the unpitying storm beat on. The ice was driven in from the flats to the wharves and piled up on the lower part of Water Street.

The lighthouses were at one time considered in danger, as the water flowed above the blockings on which they were placed, even at an hour which should have been low tide. Of one hundred and thirty vessels in port, forty-one were more or less injured; and one, the schooner Panama, was sunk at her wharf.

When, after several days, it became almost certain that no more bodies would be discovered, the stranger corpses were borne into the broad aisle of the South church, the bells tolled, and amid a concourse of two thousand five hundred people, solemn prayer was offered over these human waifs, untimely thrown upon our shores. But they were not all strangers.

Other wrecks have there been before and since December 1839; but none the circumstances of which were more indelibly impressed upon the mind, especially of those who participated in these funeral services.

On Christmas day, 1850, was discovered on the snow-covered beach, the frozen body of a young man, belonging to the schooner Argus, wrecked a day or two before. He was quite young, not more than 19 or 20, and had evidently reached the shore alive, but benumbed with cold, and exhausted with his efforts to reach the shore, had laid down in a posture of repose. He was discovered by a Mr. Johnson, of Rowley, and brought up to town by S. T. Payson, Esq. The corpse, decently arrayed for the grave, with another of the same crew, subsequently found on the beach by Mr. T. G. Dodge, was buried from the same church whence the crew of the *Pocahontas* had been carried to their last resting place. Of the crew of the Argus, five perished; two were washed off the vessel and not recovered. It is supposed the two found on the beach attempted to swim to shore. One was not accounted for; the captain only was saved.

Four months and a half later, on April 15, 1851, commenced another storm which is now fresh in the recollection of all, but which is recorded as not without interest for the future. On Monday, the slowly gathering, but thick easterly mist, announced the coming of a storm; the mist in a few hours turned to a steady rain, accompanied by a heavy gale, Tuesday greatly increasing in violence; and by Wednesday morning, it proved one of the most severe ever experienced in this vicinity. It was the more fearful, as coming on an unusually high course of tides, which rendered every additional impetus, dangerous and destructive.

At Wednesday noon, the tide was higher than at any other previously recorded, except perhaps one which occurred exactly a hundred years ago, in 1753, when during a violent northeasterly storm of snow, the tide rose to an unprecedented height, so much so that in a corn mill situated on Parker River, some six or seven miles from the seashore, the tide flowed into the depth of twenty-three inches on the floor. It was twenty-two inches higher than in the gale of December 1839, and thirteen inches higher than at any subsequent time.

Several workshops and outbuildings were grasped by the advancing waters, and borne oil in triumph, only to be cast back again, shattered and in fragments, by the next returning wave. A view of the scene the next day, made the destruction appear quite as impressive as during the violence of the storm. The road was torn up, and impassable for horses or carriages, strewn with wood and timber and fragments of buildings which the angry waves had left, as if in contempt for their worthlessness.

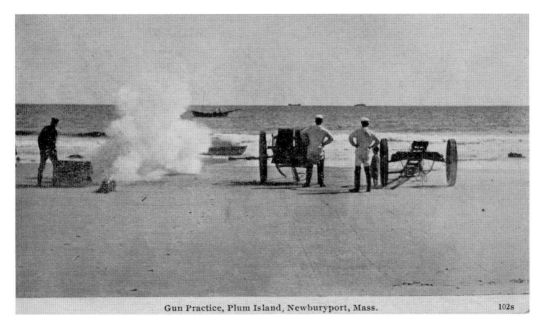

Gun Practice, Plum Island, Newburyport, Mass.   102s

Life-saving crews once used the Lyle gun, which sent out a line powered by a short-barreled cannon. The line would be directed at struggling vessels close to shore, then hauled in by a team on the beach. (*Newburyport Archival Center of the Newburyport Public Library*)

LIFE-SAVING CREW—PLUM ISLAND, NEWBURYPORT, MASS.

Members of an early life-saving crew on Plum Island. (*Newburyport Archival Center of the Newburyport Public Library*)

Many families on the lower side of the street, fearing for the foundations of their dwellings, had temporarily abandoned them, and spent the night with hospitable neighbors. Many had removed some of their more frail and valuable pieces of furniture, and for days after might be seen carrying them back to their still undemolished homes. When within the town the resistless tides had so completely pronounced their ascendency, it may well be imagined that Plum Island presented a still more desolate aspect.

On Wednesday noon, Plum Island bridge was covered with water and quite impassable; but previous to the highest rising of the tide, two of our citizens, Messrs. T. G. Dodge and O. Rundlett, impressed with the idea that a vessel was lying off Plum Island, and that it was possible they might be of use to the endangered crew, had made their way to the island at about half-past ten in the morning. There lying to, outside of the breakers, was a brig, which it was evident could not long withstand the sea, which was forcing her on to the beach. Messrs. Dodge and Rundlett made for the "Relief Hut, No. 1;" a house erected shortly before by Captain Nicholas Brown and others, for the purpose of affording temporary shelter to shipwrecked mariners, and also for those who ventured to their assistance, the latter needing occasional shelter from the fury of the storms, and the means of making a fire, to enable them to be of much assistance to those threatened with destruction. The vessel now in sight was not far from the house, and presently the watchers saw her mainsail give way. Control over her was lost, and they knew she must soon strike.

They had not long to wait. She struck almost as soon as they came opposite to her, on a reef about two hundred yards from the shore, and about half a mile below the

Postcards like this one were sent around the country in the late nineteenth and early twentieth centuries. (*Newburyport Archival Center of the Newburyport Public Library*)

relief house, and between that and the Emerson rocks. The crew could plainly see their unknown friends on the shore, and by signal communicated with them, the brig gradually beating up the beach.

Many persevering efforts were made to secure a line which the crew endeavored to throw on shore from the brig, but, undiscouraged, Messrs. Dodge and Rundlett remained in the surf nearly three hours before this was accomplished. A little before one o'clock, they were joined by Mr. Lufkin, who resided on the island, some two miles below the wreck, who with a hired man came to their assistance. An hour's more toil and the rope was at last secured, and the Captain and crew, with a single passenger, nine persons in all, were thus, by the humane and persevering efforts of these men, rescued from their perilous situation.

Too much credit cannot be given to those who thus exposed themselves to wet and cold, and exhausting endeavors to rescue the imperiled strangers. The brig proved to be the Primrose, Captain Bokman, with a cargo of coal, bound to Boston. The captain had not been able to take an observation for several days, and supposed himself in Boston Bay, till he discovered the breakers at his feet. She lay imbedded in the sand till the ensuing July, when she was towed off, having had her cargo taken out by the steamer C. B. Stevens, then running on the river between Newburyport and Haverhill.

The damage caused by this storm along the wharves and among the shipping, could not have been less than twenty thousand dollars, while the injury to the Plum Island turnpike and bridge was only repaired at a cost of about four thousand dollars. The sea at one time broke completely over the island, in some parts, leaving lakes and ponds in unwanted places when the storm subsided.

3

Early Hotels Fostered a Vibrant Social Life on the Beach

From maritime disaster to seaside tourism, here are more excerpts from the late Nancy Weare. A long-time teacher on the North Shore, Weare died in 2017. As a summer resident for many years, she watched the island change. Plum Island today is awash with people who want to live near the sea, the shore, and the river. Some visitors are seasonal guests. Others live on the island on a full-time basis. Since 2006, when water and sewer lines were extended to the island, many homeowners live in large year-round dwellings that overlook the ocean or the basin. The following excerpts are from Weare's book, *Plum Island: The Way It Was.*

Plum Island in the seventeenth and eighteenth centuries could be reached by boat, but it was too isolated to attract large numbers of people.

The first attempt to promote Plum Island as a resort came in 1806 when a group of Newburyport businessmen formed a corporation to build a bridge over Plum Island River and a toll road from the corner of Ocean Avenue to the Center. In late fall of that year a small hotel was erected near the beginning of Old Point Road, and it is believed that the construction workers were housed there.

Old newspaper accounts indicate that for many years the toll road was used primarily by guests of the hotel and by farmers who took their hay wagons across on their way to the salt marshes.

The hotel, under the management of Benjamin Clifford, quickly attracted summer visitors and sportsmen, but its function as a hostelry was interrupted briefly during the War of 1812 when it served as a barracks for soldiers stationed on the island. It soon returned to its original function, and for several decades the hotel remained the only significant non-government building at the northern end of the island.

Access to the island was not always easy despite the new road. In severe weather the bridge over Plum Island River was highly vulnerable. It was destroyed during a great storm in 1832 and was not rebuilt for several years. In order to transport guests to the hostelry, a canal was dug from the river to the hotel, and ferry service was provided.

The Plum Island Hotel was a popular destination for hunters and fishermen. (*Newburyport Archival Center of the Newburyport Public Library*)

In 1827 Moses Pettingell purchased all of the land at the north end of Plum Island from the Proprietors of Newbury with the exception of the government lot containing the lighthouses and the land occupied by the hotel complex. His purchase price of $600 was soon recouped from the sale of timber cut down on the island and from the ongoing sale of sand, which was in demand for use in the building trade.

In 1883 a dike was constructed across the entrance to the Basin. The objective was to prevent the Merrimack River from reverting to its original outlet, which is believed to have been near the head of the Basin. One effect of the dike was to create a new and safe swimming area at all times of tide. The dike remained functional for years but was not kept in repair.

The construction of the jetties at the mouth of the river commenced in 1881, and for a number of years the area was the scene of great activity. The purpose of the jetties was to increase the depth of the water at the river's mouth and to prevent the accumulation of sand on the bar. The plans called for two stone jetties to be built, each fifty feet wide at the base and fifteen feet wide at the top. Both jetties were to be at least four feet above the surface of the water at high tide. The north jetty was to be extended nearly one-half mile in a southeasterly direction from Salisbury Beach, and the south jetty was to run in a northeasterly direction from Plum Island to within a thousand feet of the north jetty.

Work began in April 1881, when the first load of rubble was dumped to form the base of the north jetty. The south jetty was started in 1883, and the work continued with many delays over a period of years until 1900, when the original jetties were completed. The stone was brought to the mouth of the river in barges, most of it from Rockport

2   Ocean Front, Plum Island, Newburyport, Mass.

Umbrellas were brought to the beach by those who did not want to be burned by the sun. (*Newburyport Archival Center of the Newburyport Public Library*)

although some stone came from the quarry opposite Carr's Island in the Merrimack. In 1914 the north jetty was extended, and in 1932 both jetties required work to overcome settling. Additional repairs were made in the 1960s. The effectiveness of the jetties has been a subject of controversy over the years, but they remain a familiar landmark on the island and attract many fishing enthusiasts.

Although for years there were accommodations for the public only at the hotel, Plum Island was a favorite destination for people from upriver who came by wagon, private boat or steamer to picnic or camp, often bringing their own tents with them. Mrs. E. Vale Smith in her book *History of Newburyport* describes a familiar scene at the island: "... the sandy beach dotted with tents, the cloth spread on the clean yellow sand, surrounded with groups of young men and maidens, old men and children, the complacent pastor, the grave deacon, all enjoying together a day of unrestrained mirth and healthful recreation...." [Author's note: This passage was included in an earlier chapter].

Steamboats, which first appeared on the Merrimack in 1828, made it possible for increasingly large numbers of people to enjoy the river and the beaches at its mouth. By the summer of 1876 there were as many as ten steamers running the river, carrying passengers from as far away as Lawrence and Haverhill. Some of these operated on a regular schedule, stopping along the way to pick up passengers bound for Newburyport, Black Rocks or Plum Island. There was also a ferry service that carried passengers between Plum Island Point and Salisbury Beach.

Fred Parsons, a local historian, described Plum Island as he remembered it in the middle 1870s:

> In our early sojourning there, the number of cottages on the Point could be counted on the fingers of one hand. There stood the government house and lighthouse just where it stands today. To the south of the lighthouse and near the Basin was another building of fair size and bearing the imposing title of Bay View House. Three little cottages stood side by side between the river opening and the government lighthouses. Farther out toward the ocean front stood what was called the "Bug Light."

The building of private cottages began in the fall of 1880 when Michael Hodge Simpson, a Newburyport native and Boston merchant, built a large summer home. This imposing cottage, located on a high dune just south of the Center, still commands attention. For many years the Pettingells had done little with their land beyond the selling of sand at the Point to Boston construction companies that sent old schooners, called droghers, to load and transport the sand to Boston. In the 1880s, the Pettingells began to offer lots for lease, and within a decade scores of camps and cottages were built, many of them substantial. The Pettingell leases contained one restriction, however: no alcoholic beverages could be sold.

By the 1880s road traffic had greatly increased. Barges (horse-drawn omnibuses) met the horsecars at Market Square to transport people to the island, and many individuals went by private conveyance. In 1883 the Newburyport Herald reported that "over two hundred carriages passed over the Plum Island turnpike, and a thousand or more (people) gathered on the sands" for a West Newbury outing held at the island.

COTTAGES AND LIGHT HOUSE, PLUM ISLAND. MASS.

A train service started in downtown Newburyport and traveled out to Plum Island. (*Newburyport Archival Center of the Newburyport Public Library*)

The hotel, which was not part of the Pettingell holding, continued to be the focal point of the northern end of the island and over the years underwent a number of additions. During its one hundred and seven years of existence the hotel had many managers, one of the earliest being Captain Nicholas Brown, a highly respected mariner whose presence attracted many of his seafaring colleagues. During his tenure the hotel staff was always prepared to offer shelter and assistance to shipwrecked sailors. Another notable manager was William Thompson, father of the local photographer W.C. Thompson. During his management the hotel was a mecca for sportsmen and became renowned for its game dinners, so much so that a piazza and a two-story ell were added, the ground floor containing a new dining room. People often came from great distances by horse and carriage to dine there. Mr. Thompson also initiated a coach service to pick up passengers at the Newburyport railroad station at 9:00 a.m. and 2:00 p.m. daily during the summer months.

In 1886 the Plum Island turnpike, bridge and hotel were sold to E.P. Shaw, a local businessman and entrepreneur. Mr. Shaw immediately built a horsecar railway line from the hotel to the Point in order to connect with the steamers of the People's Line, also under his ownership. The following spring, tracks were laid the length of Plum Island turnpike linking Plum Island to Newburyport and beyond.

The new horsecar railway line made its first trip on May 9, 1887, carrying fifty invited guests as passengers. The sidewalks of the south end of Newburyport were lined with people cheering with excitement as the four open horsecars went by. The coming of the trolley line marked a new era for Plum Island, making it accessible to anyone who

Amenities for the public included a theater. (*Newburyport Archival Center of the Newburyport Public Library*)

wished to spend a day at the beach. The trip from Market Square to the Center took twenty minutes and cost five cents. Many families now spent vacations and even whole summers at the island, since the regularly scheduled and frequent trips made it possible to commute to work.

The horsecar line was a great success. In a letter to the editor of the Newburyport Daily News a reader stated: "I have seen as many as twelve or fourteen open horsecars, with seats running crossways, and running boards on either side the entire length jammed to the limit, leave Market Square for Plum Island Hotel."

The horsecar line ran until 1895 when it was sold and then replaced by an electric railway in 1897. The electric cars served for two decades as the primary means of conveyance to Plum Island and still evoke fond memories for old-timers. For a while, travel by trolley and by steamboat overlapped, but shortly after the turn of the century, the steamboats were no longer able to compete financially, and they soon disappeared from the river. The trolleys survived until 1922 when the tracks were taken up and rail service was replaced by buses and private automobiles.

The hotel itself had been enlarged into a much more impressive structure in 1885 under the management of Mr. D. H. Fowle. The addition of another story and tower increased its capacity to forty-eight rooms, and the Newburyport Herald assured readers that it was now "a la mode." With the arrival of the trolley, the hotel prospered and was the scene of many business and civic functions.

For entertainment there was bowling in a building opposite the hotel. There were also band concerts followed by dancing, and the latter became such an attraction that a pavilion was built nearby on the ocean front. Among the orchestras that played at the Pavilion in 1905–6 was Bill Hardy's, whose song "Won't You Be My Little Sister, Louisa?" was a great hit. Also, at the Center, and independent of the hotel, there were a theater, a small restaurant, and a grocery store.

Although the hotel at the Center was by far the largest hostelry on Plum Island, there were two other small hotels at the Point. Bay View House, one of the first buildings on the island, was renowned for its clambakes, relished by upriver excursionists who arrived at the nearby steamer dock. The proprietor, George Torrey, also ran the ferry from Plum Island to Salisbury. Another hotel that was famed for its shore dinners in the early 1900s was the Oliver House on the present Northern Boulevard. Oliver House was originally built at Black Rocks and moved across the river by barge during the late 1890s.

In 1913 the Center suffered the first of two devastating fires that occurred in consecutive years. On the afternoon of July 9, a fire started beneath the platform of the refreshment booth run by Charles Noyes. Fanned by a strong southwest wind, the flames soon engulfed the Noyes buildings and the grocery store beside them. Despite the efforts of Captain Maddock of the Life Saving Station and the help of many volunteers, the blaze swept across the trolley tracks, igniting and leveling the Pavilion and a double cottage on an adjoining lot. The musicians at the Pavilion were able to rescue all their instruments except the piano, but little else could be saved. That same evening, at about ten o'clock, a fire destroyed half the length of the wooden bridge, stopping all land traffic and forcing the temporarily marooned island residents to come and go by boat. Both fires were attributed to the careless disposal of cigarettes or matches.

Less than a year later, on the morning of May 21, 1914, disaster struck the recently renovated hotel. Thomas Barney, who had just bought the property, and his staff were

Newburyport, Mass. - Steamer "Carlotta", Grape Island

The *Carlotta* was a powerboat that took visitors along the river and to Plum Island. (*Newburyport Archival Center of the Newburyport Public Library*)

in residence preparing for the season's opening. When the chef, Frank Dyer, entered the kitchen to start breakfast, he was not alarmed by a faint smell of smoke because he knew that a fire in the kitchen range had been allowed to die out overnight. When he returned from outside with a fresh supply of wood, crackling sounds from the storeroom above and thick smoke seeping into the kitchen made him realize that a fire was spreading rapidly. He raced from room to room to waken the occupants, all of whom escaped safely.

Although the hotel was not replaced, a new dance hall was built in 1915 by Paul Currier, and for many years it attracted hundreds of young people who wanted an evening of dancing. An old-timer who frequented it recalled that "a thousand paid admissions on a Saturday night was not unusual." The charge for a couple was ten cents per dance "under the crystal ball," and there were also performances by professional dancers. One of the orchestras to play at the dance hall was that of Roy Smith, a long-time resident of the island and builder of the Beachcomber at the Center.

On May 18, 1933, this dance hall, by then the property of Michael Twomey and John (Jack) Kelleher, was also destroyed by fire. Mr. Kelleher, who later became mayor of Newburyport, replaced it with a new ballroom called "Jack-O-Land," offering roller skating during the week and an orchestra for dancing on the weekends.

In 1920 the heirs of Moses Pettingell agreed to sell their Plum Island land to J. Sumner Draper of Milton, Massachusetts. The property, except for fifty acres deeded to the U.S. Government at the northerly end, was later that same year sold to the Plum Island Beach Company for the purpose of development. At the time of the sale, this part of the island contained approximately three hundred and fifteen houses for which the owners were paying a modest land rent. Writing in the *Newburyport Daily News*, Roy Smith said,

In the late nineteenth century, a pavilion offered dancing and later, roller-skating. (*Newburyport Archival Center of the Newburyport Public Library*)

Parts of Reservation Terrace at the north end of Plum Island are characterized by dunes and seashore. (*Steve Atherton Collection*)

"If you lived on the Old Point Road-side of the Basin, you paid $5 a year. On the west side of the plank-walk or car track, you paid $10 and on the ocean side of the car track, you paid $13 a year."

The new company proceeded to survey the land, laying out lots and streets. A valuation was placed on each lot, and owners of cottages were given the opportunity to purchase the land or to sell their cottages to the corporation. Not everyone was enthusiastic about the new development. The lots were small, and many of the cottage owners who had previously taken for granted their open space and ocean views now found themselves surrounded by new cottages.

That was a century ago. Plum Island now has about 1,200 residences, and thousands come "from away" each summer to enjoy the island.

4

Popularity, Density of Plum Island Has Increased in Past Two Decades

This is an article I wrote for *The Daily News* of Newburyport in 2014 that looks back on Plum Island on the 250th anniversary of the city. Consider it an update of the fine historians represented here, including E. Vale Smith and Nancy Weare. I was a reporter with *The Daily News* of Newburyport from 2012–2017. Several chapters in this book, including chapters 6, 7 and 8, are based on articles I wrote for the newspaper.

With warm weather coming, the magic name of Plum Island moves into the imaginations of locals and tourists alike. The beach, marshes and basin have been popular destinations for as long as Newburyport has been a community.

Some elements relating to the natural exposure of the island, of course, haven't changed much. Maritime engineers today are working to fortify the jetties as they did 100 years ago, so vessels can pass more easily through the river's mouth; houses built close to the water are still being buffeted by high winds, vigorous tides and the resulting erosion and reconfiguration of the beach.

But in other ways, much has changed. Larger homes are under construction; the last empty parcels are being claimed. What was once a collection of informal seasonal cottages has evolved into a community that includes many million-dollar, year-round residences.

Also, access to the water is not as universal as it once was. A century ago, families would take public transportation to the beach and spend the day near the ocean or basin; in the summer evenings, young men and women would flock to hotels and pavilions for dinner, drinking and dancing. Today Plum Island is a retreat characterized by many large homes and diminishing acreage of public beaches.

Whatever the boundaries, Plum Island is still a very popular retreat, in the visitor's mind or on the GPS. Historians say that the island was visited in 1614 by the famous Captain John Smith, but not named at the time. The island was included in a 1621–1622 land grant to Captain John Mason by the settlement president and council of Plymouth. It was dubbed "Plumb Island" because of the many beach-plum shrubs on the shore, and the shorter spelling eventually prevailed. For the first 150 years or so, settlements in Newbury, Rowley and Ipswich used the area for pastureland or perhaps fishing. The salt hay there was valued for mulching and insulation. Most of Newbury's land was

Salt hay has been gathered for more than a century, and still is today. (*Newburyport Archival Center of the Newburyport Public Library*)

held in common by the freeholders, but in 1769, municipal leaders in Newbury and Newburyport joined together to share the cost of a hospital for those with smallpox.

This was one of the first "joint ventures" of the two communities, as they had separated in 1764. The hospital, or Pest House as it was called, was located on the north end of the island to make it accessible to arriving ships who sent sick crew members to quarantine. Supervisors were serious. If a patient left before treatment was complete, Newburyport authorities were quoted as saying, "If you should come away before you are cleansed and your cloths shifted, the People in Town will stone you out again." As shipping increased along the coast, a group of private citizens got together in 1783 to fund "range lights to guide incoming ships."

These beacons were later replaced by small wooden lighthouses and a keeper's dwelling, aided in part by efforts of the Newburyport Marine Society, started in the late 18th century. In about 1829, work teams attempted to increase the depth of the water at the bar at the mouth of the Merrimack by constructing of a breakwater. Congress approved $32,000 for the task.

That appears to be the first of numerous attempts to alter the entrance and deepen the river's mouth. Many of the early reports of life on the island relate to maritime disasters. The number of wrecks off Plum Island is hard to imagine now, but in an era before ships had motors to propel them out of raging gales and wild seas, ships would often be driven onto the beach with lives lost.

A report in the *Boston Evening Transcript* in December of 1849 said:

Schooner *Nancy* of Wiscasset, with a cargo of bricks bound to Boston, went on shore on Plum Island and has entirely gone to pieces. A considerable quantity of female

Mariners have appreciated a light at Plum Island for many years. (*Newburyport Archival Center of the Newburyport Public Library*)

wearing apparel, furniture, bedding, and a letter to a lady in Boston drifted ashore from the wreck. There was no one on board, and all hands are presumed lost.

A year later, also in December, *The Daily Atlas* of Boston wrote:

On Monday, during a gale, a schooner was driven ashore on Plum Island, and was almost immediately torn to pieces by the sea, … the crew were seen from the shore, struggling in the breakers, but no assistance could be rendered to them, and they all perished. Five of their bodies have been picked up from the beach but as yet, no clue has been found to ascertain any of their names or that of their vessel.

Yet if Plum Island was the recipient of shipwrecks that came up from the sea, it was also recognized as a seaside resource that could be an asset for those willing to stay on land. Weare wrote:

The first attempt to promote Plum Island as a resort came in 1806 when a group of Newburyport businessmen formed a corporation to build a bridge over the Plum Island River and a toll road from the corner of Ocean Avenue to the Center. A small hotel was erected near the beginning of Old Point Road.

Most early users of the bridge, which was private, were either tourists or farmers traveling to the salt marshes. This bridge was destroyed in a storm in 1832 but rebuilt more than once over the years. The desire to develop useful jetties, meanwhile, was another recurring project in Plum Island history. In 1881, a load of rubble was dropped

Strong winds and high seas are part of life on Plum Island. (*Bryan Eaton photo*)

at the north end. After many delays, jetties north and south were completed in 1900. In 1914, the north jetty was extended and in 1932, both sides were refurbished. Additional repairs were made in the 1960s.

Here in 2014, the U.S. Army Corps of Engineers has helped local officials acquire almost $20 million in federal money to continue the time-honored task of fortifying the jetties. Jetties aside, residents from "upriver" started discovering the island as a retreat in the mid-19th century.

Weare says that by 1876, there were "as many as 10 steamers running the river, carrying passengers from as far away as Lawrence and Haverhill." Horse-drawn buses left from Market Square to transport people to the island. In 1883, the Newburyport Herald reported "over 200 carriages passed over the Plum Island Turnpike and a thousand or more gathered on the sands" for an outing on the island. A destination for much of the 19th century was Plum Island Hotel. In addition to hosting vacationers, the hotel became a destination for duck hunters and fishermen.

By 1885, the hotel had expanded to 48 rooms. Other hotels included the Bay View House and the Oliver House. The latter was built on Black Rocks in Salisbury and moved across the river by barge. It was demolished just several years ago. The building of private cottages began about in 1880, historians say. Transportation was the key to delivering newcomers. The horsecar line ran until 1895 when it was replaced by an electric railway in 1897. A private road from Rolfes Lane to the island was made public in 1906. The trolleys ran until about 1922, when the tracks were taken up and rail service was replaced by buses and private autos. When middle-class families began owning cars, the island became a major destination on the North Shore.

But catastrophe could occur on land as well as on the sea. In 1914 the Plum Island Hotel burned down, and in 1933 the Pavilion also was destroyed by fire. But development continued. Construction on a macadam road now called Northern Boulevard began in 1920. Cottages evolved into year-round homes, as middle-class families began building small residences. The island was also discovered by emerging naturalists.

In 1929, a philanthropist named Annie Hamilton Brown of Stoneham left money ($100,000) in her will to the Federation of Bird Clubs of New England for a wildlife sanctuary on the south end of the island. By the mid-1930s, almost 1,500 acres had been acquired by the federation, which merged with the Massachusetts Audubon Society. In 1942, the sanctuary land was turned over to the federal government and it became known as the Parker River National Wildlife Refuge.

However, hunters and fishermen were concerned that they would lose access. They wanted to shoot fowl, not admire them. Much litigation took place in the '40s, as hunters attempted to "claw back" acreage designated for a refuge. The controversy reached the desk of President Harry Truman. He brokered a compromise in about 1948.

In 2021, hunting is still permitted; fishing remains enormously popular. The refuge is almost 4,700 acres.

A summer camp known as Camp Sea Haven for polio patients operated from 1947–1988, but that facility, as many others, has slipped into history. Today the southerly, "pristine" end of the island is known as the Parker River National Wildlife Refuge. Each year it draws thousands of birders and nature lovers. Among its well-known inhabitants are the nasty greenhead fly and the lovable piping plovers.

In 2003, another controversy erupted on the island. State health officials had directed local leaders to develop a new water and sewer system to the island. Many residents objected to the state telling them how to run their island. Others were angered that they would have to pay $22,000 or more to hook into the new sewer and water system. Many angry meetings took place between 2003 and 2006 but the state was firm in its directive that Plum Island must have sewer and water connected to the mainland. The system was built. But after about a decade, problems emerged.

In 2015, heavy snow disabled many parts of Plum Island's sewer and water system. It appears that the harshness of winter and the saline tides of the Atlantic have been factors in the apparent breakdown of parts of the system.

By 2021, the expensive underground project has been in place for less than two decades, but city, state and federal officials have declared that some of its parts are ineffective and/or crumbling.

That the weather, the sea and the power of nature are factors in island lore is no surprise. Chaos stimulated by nature has always been a leading player in the Plum Island saga.

5

Two Civilizations Exist on One Barrier Island

Northern End Hosts Houses, Shops, Beaches, and Fishing Areas

The two ends of Plum Island are remarkably different. In the north, there are residences large and small, along with some commerce. In the southern portion, the uninhabited Parker River National Wildlife Refuge hosts some of the best birding sites in the nation.

In the northern sector, close to 1,200 residences crowd on to about 40 percent of the island. In recent years, the houses have been getting larger. Most structures built now cost more than $1 million.

Almost all building lots are occupied, but aggressive contractors and/or buyers often buy small cottages and replace them with larger, more grandiose structures.

Though one might read in a textbook that displacing dunes with houses will destabilize the coastline, few regulations exist to restrain builders from digging into the dunes. There is a curious disconnect on Plum Island when it comes to dunes.

Several years ago, I did a story on a fourth-grade class in Newburyport that traveled to Plum Island to plant dune grass. The reason for a day at the beach was to add grasses to ensure the strength of the dunes.

Yet on that same day, backhoes were digging into a dune on the Newbury side of the island in preparation for construction of a large house. The dune and its grasses were ravaged.

The town of Newbury appears to be supportive of any building that will provide property-tax revenue. I once asked a planning official in Newbury how it feels to approve building permits that remove dunes. He said, "We hold our noses, and vote yes."

Newbury gets about 24 percent of its annual revenue from property taxes associated with Plum Island. Newburyport realizes 6 percent of its budget from the island, according to the recent figures.

Over the years, the island has been battered by ferocious storms and threatening high tides, but many homeowners can get subsidized federal flood insurance. The insurance is relatively inexpensive and abets the decision to occupy a house on the ocean or the basin.

Some homeowners have piled boulders in front of their residences (lower left), in an attempt to keep back the ocean. (*Courtesy photo*)

Sandals left on a rock suggest visitors are walking barefooted along the shore.

The center in Newbury has offered a snack bar for many years.

About a decade ago, the federal flood insurance program was suspended because it was causing the federal government a great deal of money to pay for the storm damage. Indeed, after Hurricane Sandy hit the upper East Coast, claims totaling billions made it clear that this flood insurance program was very costly, and so, it was "suspended."

However, wealthy homeowners objected. I attended a hearing among island residents and federal officials in Lynn in about 2015 and heard comments like, "I was paying $2,000 with the federal program and now it is up to $15,000. What's that about?"

Wealthy people can be articulate. They met with elected officials and lobbied hard to reinstate the cut-rate program. It was reinstated.

There was some justification to do so. At the hearing in blue-color Lynn, some homeowners of moderate means complained they would have to sell their houses because they could not afford the market prices of insurance. Part of the federal flood plain includes neighborhoods of modest dwellings.

In general, though, the federal flood insurance program has been a cut-rate deal for those who can afford waterfront mansions.

Why do people live on a vulnerable barrier island? For many, the answer is simple. It is the best place to be on the North Shore.

The views of the ocean and river from Plum Island are spectacular. If you live there, you are an inhabitant of a charming paradise. The views are breathtaking. The ambiance

Boulders brought in for protection in recent years have become part of the seascape. (*Bryan Eaton photo*)

Many residences along the basin are protected from nor'easters that threaten houses close to the oceanfront.

is charming. Even those who inhabit dwellings with no water view love the island. The beach is close, and the summer dwellers are friendly.

One of the frustrations of non-islanders, however, is the difficulty of accessing the water. Photos from a century ago show hundreds of intown residents enjoying a day on the beach or the old postcards depict families frolicking in the basin.

Yet in 2021, parking on most public roads is prohibited. Indeed, a cottage industry in the construction of signs seems to have evolved because there are scores of metal messages declaring, "No Parking, Towaway Zone."

When I was with *The Daily News*, I often answered phone calls from chagrined visitors who had received parking tickets. "I was just bringing the wife and the four kids to the beach," said one angry resident of blue-collar Lawrence. "I got a ticket for close to $100."

I replied, "I am sorry to hear that. Did you call the police department [in Newbury] to question it?"

"Yes," the caller said. "And the cop at the other end said I was lucky that I wasn't towed."

There are paid parking lots in Newbury and Newburyport. Parking costs close to $20 (lower for residents of Newburyport), and there are a couple dozen free spots off the Plum Island Turnpike.

Yet on a hot day, there is little chance of scoring free parking in the northern sector of the island. This rankles residents, also known as taxpayers.

Yet some Plum Island residents are reaching out. In recent years, islanders host a music weekend where small bands play on porches and front yards. The whole community, including inlanders, is invited. Visitors can park at the Plum Island Airport and take a shuttle to the nearby island. Also, a sign welcoming visitors has been erected at the center in Newbury.

Regarding the costs of maintaining public services on the island, many inlanders say Plum Island residents are quick to ask for local, state and federal financial assistance after storms, but island residents do not appear to want "taxpayers" parking on the narrow roadways of their beloved island.

In retrospect, one of the notable aspects of the aforementioned water and sewer systems is that they do not work very well. In 2015, as is noted in other parts of this book, the lines froze. It was reported that the engineering company that planned the transition had chosen systems that had never been used in such a northern climate. Planners had not counted on the pipes being disabled by cold weather.

As a journalist and Newburyport resident, I was amazed such errors could happen at a high level. Where were the capable adults when the planning was being done?

Newburyport Mayor Donna Holaday, a lawyer, was not around for the planning but she was successful in "clawing back" several million dollars from the responsible engineering company to pay for repairs. Even in 2021, high tides were threatening the sewer lines on parts of the island.

Such blunders keep Newburyport in the news. Sewage lines freeze, summer homes fall off dunes after significant erosion and the beach at Reservation Terrace is disappearing so fast that some seaside homeowners are wondering if they can last another winter.

News teams from Boston often converge on the island to document the havoc. When their tapes go national, observers from afar must think the island is the coastal version of the doomed *Titanic*.

Right: Numerous "No Parking" signs are found along the inhabited sector of the island.

Below: Some houses built in recent years near Reservation Terrace are vulnerable to the sea.

Visitors enjoy the beach in summer, including snack-seeking gulls. (*Dyke Hendrickson photo*)

The northern portion of the island contains Reservation Terrace. Part of the area is a city-owned sector that includes a large public parking lot, a playground for tots and open dunes with paths to the beach.

Many dwellings here are threatened by erosion. Some houses have received ocean water in their garages and/or basements. In 2021, homeowners were fervently asking for more city, state, and federal support in helping hold back the Atlantic.

They have received support. Then-Mayor Donna Holaday approved sandbags and other "obstacles" to be put at the high-tide mark to hold back the sea. In late 2021, for instance, a "sandbag" program costing close to $450,000 was approved. This funding came largely from a state grant, and a smaller municipal contribution. Many "inland" residents wonder why tax money is being directed to support these homeowners.

Island homeowners respond by saying that they pay property taxes. Also, having a healthy Plum Island generates millions of dollars on the North Shore from rentals, shopping, and dining.

Some inlanders, though, make the argument that the homes shouldn't have been built in the first place. Indeed, conversations all over inland Newburyport since major storms in 2013 have questioned why building permits were granted for homes with exposure to the unpredictable sea.

It should be noted that the sandbagging tactic has not worked. Several years ago, plastic bags were battered, and the plastic coverings drifted into the sea.

Most homes on Plum Island are not in peril from flooding, but a study released in 2021 stated the rising water brought on by climate change is going to threaten hundreds of homes in coming years. So, the drama continues.

Life can be difficult on Plum Island, even if your house is not perched on a seaside dune, but people want to be there. Remember, Plum Island can be magnificent. It is a great place to be on a calm, sunny day.

Small boats can be easily launched on the basin side.

Placement of sand-filled plastic bags has been one method to keep back the Atlantic, but this effort was not successful. (*Courtesy photo*)

Some houses on Reservation Terrace now are close to the high-tide mark. (*Dyke Hendrickson photo*)

Boulders have been brought in by homeowners in Newbury. (*Courtesy photo*)

6

Plum Island North:
Efforts Increase to Halt Erosion

The following chapters (6, 7, and 8) offer several stories from *The Daily News* of Newburyport. I wrote them while covering storms and havoc in the period of 2012 to 2017. They might provide context to the reactions to storms.

Workers were hustling and backhoes were belching yesterday as men and machines labored to build enormous stone piles to shore up the dunes in front of oceanside homes here.

The introduction of heavy equipment on the beach is a departure from past approaches to protect the dunes, and rugged rock embankments and symmetrical stone walls have been created at the high tide mark from about the center groin to the south end of Fordham Way, about two-thirds of a mile stretch of beach.

The damaged dunes have undergone a stunning transformation since the nor'easter storm 10 days ago that left dozens of homes in peril and caused six to be destroyed. Homeowners have dumped and piled stones all along beach, creating a rugged barrier. Some are creating finely shaped walls; others have brought in great piles of rough stones that make the once glorious beach look quite unappealing.

There appeared to be disparate views on whether the work has the approval of the state Department of Environmental Protection. Several homeowners said they have received permission from the state DEP or "the governor." These individuals declined to give their names. But a staff member of the DEP yesterday said that no permissions have been given.

"They haven't gotten permission," said Ed Coletta, a spokesman for DEP. "The homeowners are concerned about their properties, and we aren't going to stop work from going on.

"When the storms are over for the year, we will be coming out to review what has been done. If the structures aren't in accord with regulations, they might have to take the walls down."

Coletta said that homeowners would not have to pay a penalty if they are required to remove the barriers that are being erected.

Above: Fishing parties can head for the sea from the Charos dock on the north end of the island (foreground). (*Dan Graovac photo*)

Left: This photo from 2013 shows that erosion was threatening homes. Following jetty repair several years later, sand is aggregating south of the south jetty. (*Steve Atherton Collection*)

Members of the state Department of Environmental Protection in the past have refused explicit permission for homeowners to move sand or build "hard structures" to prevent more erosion of the dunes.

But the possibility of homeowner action was always in the air.

Tracy Blais, Newbury town administrator, could not be reached for comment yesterday, nor could Joe Story, chairman of the Board of Selectmen here.

"The homeowners are paying for this, not the town," said Doug Packer, Newbury's conservation agent. He indicated town officials are not supervising the construction of the walls and barriers.

One property owner yesterday said she was relieved that the homeowners are finally acting.

"We are thankful to be able to do this, but it's too late for those who have lost their homes," said a homeowner who declined to give her name. "There has been red tape and roadblocks, and we are taking advantage of the moment now."

In recent weeks, six oceanfront residences on Annapolis Way and Fordham Way have been demolished and carted away after being condemned. That is a cost borne by the owners.

About two dozen structures are still listed as vulnerable.

Now it appears that no expense is being spared by homeowners who are trying to save what they have.

One construction worker yesterday said more than $100,000 has been spent in bringing in loose boulders and sand to fortify the dunes in front of seven houses on the southernmost end of Fordham Way.

The rock is coming from Seabrook, and the sand is being imported from northern Maine, said the worker, who declined to give his name.

At blue, an oceanside hotel on Fordham Way, massive chunks of cut stone were being placed on top of the other as a means for holding back the Atlantic. Individual sections of stone are about 6 feet by 3 feet by 3 feet.

There are currently no guests at the hotel, neighbors said.

At a recent meeting of the Merrimack River Beach Alliance, numerous homeowners expressed frustration that state officials were not giving them latitude to scrape the beach and erect hard structures to halt the erosion that threatens their homes.

State Sen. Bruce Tarr, R-Gloucester, co-chairman of the MRBA, was circumspect in his analysis at that meeting.

Tarr addressed property owners: "You can do what you need to do to save your place, but you've got to know that you might have to remove it after the fact." He was referring to rebuilding a dune or introducing a hard-structure barrier in contravention of DEP's rules.

Homeowners on the south end of Plum Island clearly have taken action to protect their property. They said they are committed to bringing in sand, dune grass or other elements to ensure the beach is attractive and healthy.

7

Last "Old Hotel"
to Be Torn Down

This article first appeared in *The Daily News* in 2013.

The last surviving "old hotel" at Plum Island Point will be torn down following the approval of a demolition permit voted last week by the Historical Commission.

The Oliver House at 245 Northern Blvd. will be taken down in 2013 for safety reasons, city officials say. The empty structure is visibly sagging on the outside and apparently collapsing on the inside.

"We're not happy about approving a demolition," said Linda Smiley, who chairs the commission. "It's a piece of history, and we voted reluctantly.

"The owners investigated how it could be saved and preserved, but it just wasn't feasible. The weather on the island is tough, and even from the street it's clear that there are major problems with the structure."

The property is owned by Kevin and Deborah Raftery of Newburyport, who purchased it in 2008, according to the municipal assessor's office. They did not return calls requesting comment.

(Sentence removed)

The Oliver House opened about 1900 as a guesthouse and hotel but has been empty for several decades. It represents the last "old hotel" on the island, which had numerous overnight venues a century ago.

Local historians say Oliver House was built in Salisbury and transported by barge across the Merrimack River. Among its notable visitors was Jack Johnson, the first black heavyweight boxing champion (1908–1915).

Owners until recently were trying to sell the property. Indeed, a "for sale" sign still stands in the front yard. It was hoped that it could be restored.

Square footage of the 13-room hotel is 3,298. Cost price for the total package was $999,000, according to the website of the listing agency, but no buyers came forth to acquire the wooden structure.

The Oliver House was one of the last old hotels on Plum Island. (*Courtesy photo*)

8

Sand "Mining" Eyed as Plum Island Remedy

This article first appeared in *The Daily News* in 2013.

Plum Island residents in 2013 in Newbury seeking a sustainable solution to havoc brought on by erosion have developed a proposal for a pilot program to "mine" sand so that replenished dunes can protect seaside homes.

Marc Sarkady, who heads the Plum Island Foundation, said that drawings and engineering studies were submitted Wednesday to top officials of the Department of Environmental Protection, including DEP Commissioner Ken Kimmell. DEP officials made no decision at the session, held in state offices in Boston, but Sarkady said the decision-makers listened closely.

"This wasn't just an abstract conversation," said Sarkady, a Washington-based lawyer who has a home at 50 Northern Blvd. on the island. "DEP officials were open and responsive, and listened attentively and asked questions."

Gloucester-based state Senate Minority Leader Bruce Tarr, whose district includes Plum Island and who has been active in seeking to develop a response to erosion issues there and elsewhere, including across Cape Ann, termed the meeting "a step forward."

"Officials of the DEP heard from us that we'd like a decision as soon as possible." said Tarr, who also serves as co-chair of the Merrimack River Beach Alliance. "We had a good representation, and (engineer) David Vine and (Northeastern) Professor Peter Rosen did a good job in providing scientific information to support the mining proposal."

Mining is an exercise in which heavy equipment enters the beach at low tide and scoops up large amounts of sand. That sand is dumped near the high-tide mark in an effort to build up dunes that have been diminished by erosion.

Longtime residents of the island say this practice was carried out effectively in the late '70s. One homeowner said that in the past, seaside dwellers dug out depressions that were "big enough to bury a battleship."

But state officials discouraged the process in the late '90s, islanders say. Indeed, as frequently as three months ago, homeowners were required to apply for a state permit just to "scrape" sand toward the dunes.

Most buildable land on the northern section of the island is now taken. (*Courtesy photo*)

The idea of mining hadn't been broached until after the last significant winter storm, which fostered enough erosion-caused damage to ruin numerous houses. Six houses were destroyed and removed, and about 20 are still vulnerable.

As a result of this damage, numerous residents on the Newbury end of the island are earnestly pressing members of the DEP to permit mining as a means to sustain beaches and dunes.

All mining activity would be paid by homeowners, members of the Foundation say. The pilot program would involve mining of a 400 to 500-foot stretch of beach south of the island groin. Sarkady said that the results would be studied by local and state officials, and analysis would continue from there.

Joe Story, chairman of the Newbury Board of Selectmen, noted that the idea isn't new, adding that "it would be another tool in the bag if we could do this mining.

"It was encouraging that the DEP invited us in to talk," he added, "and we told them that we are hoping for a decision very quickly."

North Shore residents in many coastal communities are seeking new strategies to counter erosion following a winter (2013) where four storms created an unusual amount of erosion—and subsequent damage of homes. But erosion is not the only phenomenon occurring on the coast. Aerial photos show that great masses of sand have been moving off Plum Island this winter, creating new sandbars and larger beaches in some areas.

Authors of the proposal say that bulldozers and bucket loaders would be employed to gather sand at low tide and relocate it to the dunes. The number of machines that would be required has not been finalized.

9

An Outsider Looks at the
Challenges on Plum Island

The following is an excerpt from a story written in 2015 for *CommonWealth* magazine by a perceptive "off-island" writer named Gabrielle Gurley. It highlights some of the practical challenges of the island and addresses the question: "If it is a vulnerable barrier island, why do people keep building houses?"

Plum Island is one of the most spectacular places to live in Massachusetts. With high dunes and rolling beaches on the lip of the Atlantic Ocean, people move to this barrier island north of Cape Ann for a deep blue slice of paradise. But paradise can quickly turn to hell when the ocean's full fury is unleashed. A major storm hit to the island in 2013 and the nor'easter claimed six homes.

But once the big storms blow over, difficult conversations about the future of Plum Island don't tend to rise to the top of the agenda. Plum Island in many ways is a case study of climate change paralysis. Local municipal leaders, wary of tangling with beachfront property owners who provide a significant chunk of town property tax revenue, careen from crisis to crisis and the tough conversations about the future move to the back burner. State officials are also conflicted, sometimes asserting their power to address serious issues, but other times hanging back to avoid the fray when their voices might be needed. Meanwhile, competing groups of homeowners and residents push and pull the powers that be in different directions.

Plum Island is a barrier island about 11 miles long, dangling off the northeast corner of Massachusetts where the Merrimack River meets the Atlantic Ocean. The Parker River National Wildlife Refuge, created by the federal government in 1942, takes up about two-thirds of the island. Newbury and Newburyport divide the tightly packed northern end of about 1,200 homes, roughly 800 in Newbury and 400 in Newburyport. Parts of the undeveloped southern stretch of the island are located in Ipswich and Rowley.

In a geological sense, Plum Island is stable. It hasn't moved in thousands of years, according to Christopher Hein, a coastal geologist at the Virginia Institute of Marine Science at the College of William and Mary. Where some barrier islands, so-named because they protect the mainland from storms, have moved landward several miles

The views are spectacular from many homes on the island.

over eons—think of the Outer Banks of North Carolina—Plum Island has stayed put. It has also not been completely washed over by storms in a very long time.

Although the land mass has not moved in thousands of years, the visible landmarks like beaches and dunes have. The summer shores that people enjoy lying on are in a continuous process of shifting, disappearing, and reforming as wind, waves, and storms chisel and sculpt them. The tall sand dunes are shifting toward the mainland as sand gets redeposited on the back of the island among the small trees, shrubs, and other plant life that help stabilize the island. The fast-flowing Merrimack River, the second-largest river in New England, influences where the sand moves. Man-made structures such as the two jetties at the mouth of the Merrimack, as well as seawalls and groins (smaller seawalls) elsewhere, also influence the island processes. Scientists do not yet fully understand how all these factors interact. No model exists of how sand distributes itself around and on the barrier island. What is known is that the erosion on Plum Island, which seems to come and go every 25 to 40 years, is now slowly shifting southward, Hein says.

Both summer and winter storms influence the island's topography. Hurricanes tend to be fast-moving and short-lived, with Plum Island protected to some degree by Cape Ann to the south. Nor'easters are a different story. They can hit Plum Island head on from the northeast-facing open ocean and can linger and spin longer. Combine the deep erosion of the kind seen on Plum Island today with a long-lasting nor'easter and you get the dramatic spectacle of homes falling into the ocean as they did in March 2013.

Nature makes life difficult on Plum Island, but humans have complicated the picture even more. The major players on the island—lawmakers, state agencies, municipal officials and various factions of residents—weave in and out of controversy so regularly that trying to chart any type of forward motion has been difficult.

Swallows return each spring to Reservation Terrace. (*Dyke Hendrickson photo*)

Money is often a prime motivator. Like most Massachusetts cities and towns, Newburyport and Newbury are heavily dependent on property taxes. And Plum Island residents know they are sitting on a valuable part of that equation. That subtext underlines many aspects of the debate over how to manage the island and plan for its future.

Plum Island generates about $7 million in property tax revenue annually. Newbury takes in about $4 million, accounting for nearly a third of the town's total real estate taxes. Much larger Newburyport takes in about $3 million from Plum Island properties, representing about 6 percent of the city's $48 million annual tax levy.

Multi-million-dollar beachfront homes generate tens of thousands of dollars in property taxes. But what the beachfront gives, it can also take away. When storms smash homes into the sea, municipal tax revenues take a hit.

"Coastal property, particularly in a small town like Newbury, is a significant part of the [tax] base," says Sen. Bruce Tarr, a Gloucester Republican who represents Newbury. "If [a home's] value gets diminished, then what strategy does the town have to replace that value? Do you issue more building permits to let building occur in other parts of the town? Maybe allow more commercial development? The point is that the revenue to run the town has to come from somewhere."

The state has an important role to play in the ongoing debate over Plum Island's future, but it has seemed ambivalent about getting pulled too deeply into the fray. The Department of Environmental Protection has tussled with residents, particularly in Newbury, standing behind regulations to prohibit homeowners from employing temporary beach engineering techniques that the agency says make matters worse. Those tensions have strained the relationship between the agency and communities, making department officials leery of plunging into unforeseen problems.

DEP was nonetheless the force behind one of the biggest changes to come to the island in decades. As summer-only shacks on Plum Island gave way to large homes, the septic systems that the island relied on came into conflict with state sanitary regulations. Because of small lot sizes, one person's septic system might be near another person's well, leading to contamination. Concerned about the public health risks to water sources, the Department of Environmental Protection ordered Newburyport to install a water and sewer system to serve both communities. Plum Island homeowners were assessed as much as $22,000 each to pay for the $22.9 million water and sewer system that was installed in 2006.

The brutal winter of 2015, however, proved to be too much for the system and various components of it froze, leaving some Newburyport homes without running water—and an ability to dispose waste into the system—for several weeks. More than 600 homes were affected. The city had to pay for 70 hotel rooms to house residents. Plum Island Hall, the headquarters of Plum Island Taxpayers and Associates, wasn't hit by the outage and stayed open 24/7 so people could use restrooms and get updates.

But the system had already malfunctioned several times since its installation, and Newburyport and Newbury don't have the funds to repair the problems without state assistance. Newburyport Mayor Donna Holaday says that between this winter's repairs and past sewer issues and water main breaks, the system has already cost the city nearly $1 million in fixes. City officials are working with Attorney General Maura Healey's office and the Department of Environmental Protection to reach a settlement with CDM Smith, the Boston-based firm that installed the system. The state also put $30,000 into a grant for repairs and $50,000 into a study to figure out why the system does not work properly. Officials have to figure out a way to "protect the sewer and water infrastructure investment," says Doug Packer, Newbury's conservation agent.

What the sewer repair costs all mean is that expensive housing development that held the promise of boosting municipal tax revenue payments has led to strain on the same budgets it was supposed to help. And while the state set things in motion by ordering the switch to a costly sewer system, it has had little to say about the problems that have ensued.

The pros and cons of alternative visions for Plum Island boil down to three options, all of them controversial. Restoring the entire island to its natural state like the neighboring wildlife refuge is an option favored by some environmentalists. Not surprisingly, it also prompts the most passionate local opposition and is a nonstarter.

A middle-ground position is held by those who favor an idea termed a "managed retreat." That approach would focus on protecting the inhabited parts of the island that can be saved, converting the others into parks or other recreational spaces, and beefing up services that produce revenue, such as visitor parking. A transition strategy under "managed retreat" would aim to provide compensation to owners of the most vulnerable properties. Some state lawmakers believe the enactment of a voluntary buyback program would persuade owners of the properties at greatest risk or owners who've already experienced multiple losses to move on.

Some vocal homeowners support a third option. They believe that if local, state, and federal governments won't use tax dollars to protect lives and property, residents should be able to use any means necessary to protect their homes. Newbury resident Bob Connors has been engaged in a long-running war of words with the Department of Environmental

The sea takes on many colors and shades.

Plum Island can be a great place to take a walk, depending on the weather.

Protection over the measures he's used and paid for to shore up the dune in front of his beachfront home, including bringing in large boulders and scraping the beach.

Connors is a co-founder of the nonprofit Plum Island Foundation, another citizens group on the island. The Pacific Legal Foundation, a California public interest law group that "challenges government hubris in the enforcement of state environmental regulations," according to the group's website, has often backstopped the Plum Island organization in its battles with the state. Connors says the government shouldn't be allowed to make decisions about personal property based on what-if environmental scenarios. "You can't collect our taxes and deny us the very basic services that you provide everybody else," he says.

The Merrimack River Beach Alliance, founded in 2008, has emerged as the most trusted convener that can get residents, local, state, and federal agencies in the same room to constructively discuss the erosion issues in Newbury, Newburyport, and Salisbury, which has many of the same erosion problems as its neighbors. In recent comments on the draft report of the state-sponsored Coastal Erosion Commission, the alliance noted that Massachusetts should avoid coastal policies that require the removal or abandonment of any public or private buildings and infrastructure. Relocation should only be mandated when all other options have been exhausted, the group said.

Co-chaired by Tarr, the state senator, the group has successfully pursued a number of major erosion-fighting projects, including convincing the US Army Corps of Engineers to undertake more than $15 million in repairs to the jetties at the mouth of the Merrimack River. Many locals believe that the crumbling jetties, which had not been repaired since the 1970s, are largely responsible for Plum Island's severe erosion issues.

A boat heads out to sea at dawn. (*Dan Graovac photo*)

The Coastal Erosion Commission, established by the Legislature in 2013 to study and collect data on the impact of erosion on the state's coastline, may help communities understand the costs and benefits of their beach-related activities and how best to maximize and protect them. There's limited information available statewide or in places like Newburyport and Newbury. Last year, about 250,000 people visited the Parker River refuge. Newburyport takes in about $75,000 annually from its beach parking lots and the Mass Audubon's winter Merrimack River Eagle Festival, which marks the return of bald eagles to the area.

Behind the allure of a Plum Island house on dune with an ocean view is a harsh reality. Last winter, it was sewage. Two years ago, it was the loss of homes. However sensible it might seem to the risk-averse denizens of inland Massachusetts, a "managed retreat" that involves some people giving up their homes is not a popular talking point on Plum Island. But it is one that nature's fury and slim financial resources at all levels of government may wind up demanding. "Unpredictability is a very difficult thing for municipal planners," says Tarr. "We are trying to make them proactive ... the difficult thing is that we are going to have to make some difficult decisions."

10

Two Civilizations Share One Barrier Island

In Southern Sector, National Wildlife Refuge Is a Paradise for Birds and People

The southern end of Plum Island, by contrast to the northern sector, is a wildlife refuge with few human embellishments. There is a parking lot with restrooms. There are parking areas adjacent to clearings where one can view and/or photograph birds and other wildlife. As a news story in this book notes, Plum Island is the third most frequented bird-watching venue in the country.

Curiously, as the northern end of the island has steadily built up, the southern portion has divested itself of human habitation.

Since the federal government took over southern portion in 1942, residences have been torn down. A camp for polio patients was closed after the illness was eradicated. Health officials treating other diseases wanted to run it for their own patients, but the feds said no.

Thus, the Parker River National Wildlife Refuge exists as refuge for wildlife—and for residents who want to get back to nature.

This can be frustrating. Federal officials are determined to accommodate the birds. The piping plover, for instance, needs peace and quiet so pairs can breed. That often means that from April until July, much of the beach is closed to humans. There can be about three dozen "couples" in a given season but thousands of human visitors are kept off the beaches and dunes so the birds can procreate.

At the refuge, many popular activities are banned. Visitors cannot bring dogs to the beach. Noisemakers such as all-terrain vehicles are not permitted.

As a reporter, I covered a public meeting several years ago that the refuge officials had convened to discuss their work at the 4,667-acre retreat. Several visitors became frustrated.

One burly middle-aged man asked, "I want to run my dogs. Why can't I?"

Answer: "They scare the birds. This refuge exists for wildlife, not people."

Another said, "I want to hunt; I want to bring my ATV. Why can't I?"

Answer: "It is not good for the birds. This refuge exists for wildlife, not people."

The Parker River National Wildlife Refuge offers a parking lot, drinking water, and restrooms.

This beach at Sandy Point is one of the most isolated spots on Plum Island.

Each year many newcomers to Parker River are flummoxed to learn that their activities are restricted, but so it goes.

The Parker River National Wildlife Refuge hosts many educational events. Over the years, hundreds of North Shore residents have served as volunteers. People love the refuge.

Sandy Point Beach, at the southernmost part of the island, is an intriguing small state park. It is separate from the refuge. From this beach, one can see Ipswich a few hundred feet away.

The southern sector of Plum Island is a paradise for those who love the outdoors, with bicyclists and hikers abounding. The fishing can be spectacular. There is even duck-hunting under controlled conditions, and the birdwatching is some of the best in the nation.

To steal a line from an earlier section of this tome, Plum Island can be magnificent. It is a great place to be on a calm, sunny day.

11

The History of the Parker River National Wildlife Refuge

The writer-historian, Thomas R. Hamilton, was chairman of the Department of Biology at Phillips Academy in Andover, when he wrote this informal history in 1998. It is excerpted from the Searchable Ornithological Research Archive (SORA).

The Parker River National Wildlife Refuge, located 35 miles north of Boston and 6 miles east of Newburyport, Massachusetts, is a popular area visited by over 250,000 birders, swimmers, and saltwater anglers each year. The refuge consists of thousands of acres of salt marsh and 7 miles of sand dunes and barrier beach.

As part of the National Wildlife Refuge System, the area is a major resting and feeding area for migrating ducks and geese; over 300 bird species have been seen in the refuge in the last twenty years. In this article I will describe some of the geological processes that formed the island, the various ways in which the land and adjacent salt marsh have been and are being used, and the political process which formed the current boundaries of the refuge.

About 12,000 years ago, when New England was covered by the last glacier, the coastline was several hundred miles to the east of what is now Plum Island.

As the glacier retreated and the sea rose, the shoreline became a compromise between the sea and the rebounding land. At what is now the southern end of Plum Island, the glacier left behind five low hills consisting of a mixture of loose boulders, gravel, and sand. Three of these hills (Bar Head, Stage Island, Cross Farm Hill) are part of the island, and another (Grape Hill) exists as a slight rise in the salt marsh. The fifth hill, Emerson's Rocks, has severely eroded and is a now reduced to a strand of rocks that are visible on the ocean side of the southern end of the island during low tides. These landmarks can be located with a map available at the refuge headquarters.

Over the years silt from the Merrimack River and sand from the glacial deposits on the coast of New Hampshire were transported by ocean currents that move in a southerly direction and deposit their loads around the drumlins. When Plum Island became established, it formed a barrier against powerful ocean waves, causing the development of a protected area between the island and the mainland.

This quiet area accumulated silt transported by the Merrimack, Rowley, and Ipswich rivers and developed into the 3,000 acres of salt marsh that are visible from the refuge road. The nutrient-rich waters of the marsh provide productive habitat for ducks, geese, wading birds, and fish.

Native Americans traveled down the Merrimack River in the spring to establish seasonal fishing camps on Plum Island. In the 19th century, archaeologists excavated these sites and found many stone and flint tools, fragments of pottery, and several middens consisting of large piles of shells. The sites of three camps were discovered in what are now the Newbury and Ipswich sections of the island.

The first recorded sighting of Plum Island by a European was by Samuel de Champlain in 1605. In 1614, Captain John Smith mapped Plum Island and described it as an area "fit for pastures, with many faire high groves of mulberrie trees and gardens; and there is also Pines and other wood to make this place an excellent habitation." In 1637 the newly incorporated town of Newbury petitioned the General Court of Massachusetts to have Plum Island and the adjacent salt marsh annexed by the town. Since the settlers in neighboring Rowley and Ipswich also valued the salt marsh grass, they were not about to give up their right to what was viewed as common land.

Therefore, in 1646 the General Court, with the wisdom of a Puritan Solomon, divided the island and marsh among the three towns. Later, a portion of Newbury's share was transferred to Newburyport after that city was founded. In a few years the towns divided their portions into small parcels that were allotted to their respective residents; unfortunately, this started a period of uncontrolled grazing by horses, pigs, and cattle.

Since fences were nonexistent, the animals were simply turned loose on the island and marsh, destroying much of the original vegetation and starting a period of serious erosion. In 1739 an attempt was made to save the remaining vegetation and reduce erosion by curtailing the free-roaming cattle and prohibiting the cutting of trees under six inches in diameter.

Probably by this time, however, few large trees remained. Salt marsh grass is still harvested in some areas of the marsh outside the refuge. In the past, the cut grass was stacked on platforms built on two-foot-high posts to hold the drying grass well above the high-tide mark. The stacks of marsh grass were collected in the winter, when it was possible to drive horse-drawn wagons or sleds onto the marsh. Remnants of these platforms can still be seen in the marsh, especially in the area near the gatehouse.

Marsh grass was used for roofing and as bedding for cattle. This coarse plant, which grows along the banks of the Ipswich and Parker rivers, was harvested by hand from shallow-draft boats during low tides. By the beginning of the 19th century, many of the small holdings at the southern end of Plum Island had been consolidated into farms of approximately 100 acres. Two of these farms are remembered today in the place names of Emerson's Rocks and Cross Farm Hill. At the northern end of the island, transport to the mainland was made easier when a toll road was built through the marsh and a small bridge was built over the Plum Island River.

This was soon followed by the construction of a small hotel. By the end of the 19th century, many summer cottages, some quite large, had been built, several hotels and businesses were operating, and public transportation along a horse-car railway (later replaced by an electric trolley) from Newburyport made Plum Island a popular destination for summer day-trippers. In the early 20th century, the Plum Island Beach

The Wildlife Refuge offers numerous areas for birdwatching, including this spot at Hellcat.

An early map by explorer John Smith, pictured here. (*Courtesy graphic*)

Staffers of the Parker River National Wildlife Refuge are planning for the day when the sea rises significantly in the marsh.

Company secured title to most of the northern end of the island and quickly developed plans to create hundreds of small house lots to be offered for sale to the public. The paving of the Plum Island Turnpike and Northern Boulevard made the northern end of the island easily accessible by automobile.

Although the southern end of Plum Island was most easily visited by boat, the Bar Island Realty Company, which owned approximately 400 acres on Sandy Point, had elaborate plans for creating roads and numerous small house lots. Clearly, by the late 1930s rapid development on Plum Island was occurring. If development had been allowed to continue unchecked, in a few years the entire island would have been covered with small, seasonal dwellings, and the character of the island would have changed forever.

By the start of the 20th century, the area's importance was recognized by prominent ornithologists such as Charles W. Townsend and Edward Howe Forbush, who urged that Plum Island be secured as a bird sanctuary.

In 1929 Annie H. Brown, a long-time member of Massachusetts Audubon Society, bequeathed to The Federation of the Bird Clubs of New England a large part of her estate (close to $100,000, according to Refuge history) for the establishment and maintenance of a wildlife sanctuary. After several months of negotiations, the executors of the estate and the officers of the Federation wisely selected a parcel of 300 acres of beach, dunes and salt marsh near the southern end of Plum Island as the core of the new bird sanctuary. Soon after the initial purchase two more tracts were added, bringing the total protected area to approximately 600 acres. The officers of the Federation also secured options to purchase an additional contiguous 800 acres and immediately initiated plans to raise the necessary funds totaling $10,000.

Annie Brown, a Stoneham philanthropist, left money after she died in 1929 for birding clubs to buy land on Plum Island.

The Federation later merged with the Massachusetts Audubon Society, and by 1938 the Society had consolidated numerous small pieces of property to form the Annie H. Brown Sanctuary, which consisted of 1,115 acres. Part of Brown's bequest supported two wardens who patrolled the sanctuary to prevent trespassing by hunters. Evidently, the presence of a bird sanctuary that set aside some prime hunting areas for the preservation of wildlife was not appreciated by local hunters.

The Essex County Sportsmen's Association protested the granting of tax-exempt status to the Massachusetts Audubon Society. In an article in the September 10, 1937, issue of the *Lawrence Tribune*, the Sportsmen's Association objected to the Society's "vast holdings … allowing vermin to get out of control besides limiting the land on which hunting may be done." Judge Robert Walcott, president of Massachusetts Audubon Society, defended the expansion of the sanctuary by stating that it was established to provide "a safe resting, feeding and breeding ground for game and non-game species."

To both professional and amateur ornithologists it was obvious that Plum Island and the adjacent marsh were critical parts of the Atlantic flyway, allowing waterfowl a chance to rest and find food along their migration route. In the 1940s there was anecdotal evidence that Black Ducks, much prized by hunters, were in a serious population decline, according to writer Rachel Carson, a writer-researcher for the U.S. Fish and Wildlife Service. The Service sought to purchase the Brown Sanctuary in 1940 so that it could be a core part of a federal wildlife sanctuary.

Initially the offer was declined. However, in 1942 the Society, under threat of the land being taken by eminent domain, sold their holdings on Plum Island for $35,000 and the Parker River National Wildlife Refuge was established. Funds from the sale of the

Parts of the Wildlife Refuge can be off-limits to visitors when birds are procreating.

Brown Sanctuary were later used to help establish the Ipswich River Audubon Sanctuary in 1951. The Society agreed to the sale only if the Brown Sanctuary were to become part of a substantially larger wildlife refuge and members of the Massachusetts Audubon Society were to have access to the refuge for the purpose of bird study.

Members of the Essex County Sportsmen's Association opposed the sale of the Brown Sanctuary because they believed that it would lead to the acquisition of even more of the island and salt marsh for the establishment of a much larger federal wildlife refuge. Over the protests of local hunters, the U.S. Fish and Wildlife Service was authorized by Congress to acquire a total of 12,000 acres of marsh as well as all of Plum Island.

Local opposition was very strong, resulting in a bill passed by Congress to eliminate the refuge. Although President Truman pocket-vetoed this bill, vigorous opposition to the establishment of the refuge remained. Political pressure in Washington continued for two more years until a compromise bill was finally passed by Congress and signed by the president on June 4, 1948.

Most of the land that had been taken by eminent domain was returned to the previous owners. However, the heart of the original refuge was saved; and most of Plum Island, as well as a large area of marsh, survived as the Parker River National Wildlife Refuge. Over the years since the passage of the compromise legislation in 1948, the Fish and Wildlife Service has, with revenue generated by the sale of Duck Stamps, regained some of the land that had been given up and all but one of the private camps within the refuge boundaries have been acquired.

Today the total area of the refuge is 4,667 acres, less than half of the size originally authorized by Congress in 1941. Hunters and landowners who wanted to regain their right to freely use the marsh and beaches regained much of what had been taken by the federal government. In the process, however, a large area which could have been preserved as a resting place for migratory birds was lost.

The refuge clearly means many things to many people, and the U.S. Fish and Wildlife Service has tried hard to accommodate as many demands as possible while also meeting their legal mandate to maintain a wildlife refuge.

Shell-fishing in designated areas is permitted, as well as surf fishing between July 1 and October 31, provided the areas are not closed for nesting birds. Although it may seem contradictory, in some areas of the refuge waterfowl hunting for geese, ducks, American Coot, and sea ducks is permitted in accordance with refuge, state, and federal regulations.

In 1997 a two-day deer hunt was permitted on December 1 and 2. And between Labor Day and the end of October, Beach Plum collecting occurs on the east side of the refuge road. Other than banding waterfowl, refuge personnel are not directly involved in ongoing scientific research. However, the refuge is the site of several research studies that include the banding and surveying of land birds (Massachusetts Audubon Society), a survey of the Brown-tailed Moth (Massachusetts Department of Environmental Protection), an annual hawk survey (Eastern Hawk Watch Association), a survey of mammals and vegetation (University of Vermont), a study of the genetics of beach plums (University of Vermont), and the tagging of migratory monarch butterflies (University of Toronto).

Many visitors to the refuge come to use the wide, beautiful beaches for swimming and sunbathing. In 1987, however, a large area of the beach was closed to protect the nesting area of a lone pair of piping plovers, an endangered species. Subsequently, following the federal mandate of the Endangered Species Act, the entire beach within the refuge boundary has been closed to all recreational activity from the first of April to early August.

In 1995, twenty-one pairs of piping plovers nested on the beach and produced forty-four chicks; however, in 1997 the number of nesting plover pairs was down to sixteen, and only twenty chicks were produced. During the nesting season the refuge staff of eight employees, with the help of approximately forty-five volunteer "plover wardens," patrol the beach and access points.

Often much of their time is spent patiently explaining to would-be beachgoers the necessity of keeping off the beach while the plovers are nesting. Interestingly, 80 percent of the visitors between June 1993, and May 1994, supported the beach closure. The refuge staff have worked hard to protect the piping plovers, but they have had to work against many obstacles: severe erosion to the widest areas of beach destroyed some of the best plover nesting areas, uncontrolled dogs come into the refuge from homes in the residential part of the island and from Sandy Point State Reservation, predators such as foxes, skunks, and raccoons are difficult to control because of new live-trap regulations and, sadly, wanton vandalism resulted in the destruction of one nest in 1997.

Since the establishment of the refuge, the dunes and salt marsh have gradually started to return to a more "primitive" condition, while the surrounding countryside has gone through a tremendous house-building boom, putting a higher premium on the remaining open spaces. Although people come to the refuge for many reasons, a survey of visitors suggests that 39 percent come for the purpose of wildlife observation, helping to support the notion that Plum Island is the most heavily birded area in Massachusetts.

Many visitors come simply to see the flocks of migrating geese or the astounding numbers of tree swallows that gather in late August. In the winter Snowy Owls, Rough-legged

Waterfowl are majestic—and common—at the Wildlife Refuge. (*Courtesy photo*)

Hawks, and Northern Harriers are often seen flying over the marsh. In late November, Canada Geese and Black Ducks gather in large numbers in open water, and other migrants from the north such as Snow Buntings, Lapland Longspurs, and Horned Larks are often found in large flocks among the dunes. The refuge checklist (available at the gatehouse) identifies 303 species that have been recorded on or near the refuge during the past ten years.

Since the Parker River Refuge is thoroughly birded throughout the year, any unusual vagrants that visits the area are probably going to be sighted by someone. Using records published in Bird Observer and other sources, I was able to compile the following brief list of interesting rarities sighted on or from Plum Island during the last ten years: "Eurasian" Green-Winged Teal (1988), Little Egret (1989), Terek Sandpiper (1990), Lark Bunting (1990), Gull-billed Tern (1991), Sandhill Crane (1992), Eurasian Wigeon (1993), Black-necked Stilt (1995), Ruff (1995), Vermilion Flycatcher (1995), Gyrfalcon (1996), Say's Phoebe (1996), Swainson's Hawk (1996), Long-billed Curlew (1996), Forster's Tern (1997), and American White Pelican (1997).

In 1985 the Fish and Wildlife Service took possession of a 12-acre parcel of land off Plum Island for the purpose of building a new headquarters and visitors' center. The Trust for Public Land purchased the property for $526,000 and sold it to the Fish and Wildlife Service for $430,000; the deficit was made up by a coalition consisting of the New England Chapter of the Sierra Club, The Conservation Law Foundation, and Massachusetts Audubon Society.

The Parker River National Wildlife Refuge is a mosaic of compromises and uses. The U.S. Fish and Wildlife Service has had to balance the demands of the public for access to the refuge for recreational purposes against the service's mandate to maximize wildfowl management.

Any human activity within the refuge can only be permitted if it is compatible with the overall mission of the refuge. In the words of John L. Fillio, onetime Refuge Manager, "Our first objective is wildlife, not people. This is a wildlife refuge, not a park." As the population of northeastern Massachusetts continues to grow and open spaces become fewer, the value of the refuge as a place of sanctuary for wildlife will continue to increase. This beautiful and fragile environment must be protected.

12

Through the Years:
A History of the Audubon Society

The Audubon Society has played a valuable role in the development of Plum Island as a home for both birds and nature lovers. Here is a timeline from more than a century's worth of Audubon. It is found on the website of the Audubon Society.

1896: Harriet Hemenway and Minna B. Hall organize a series of afternoon teas to convince Boston society ladies to eschew hats with bird feathers. These meetings culminate in the founding of the Massachusetts Audubon Society.

1900: Frank Chapman proposes the first annual Christmas Bird Count as an alternative to the traditional Christmas side hunt in his publication, Bird Lore, predecessor to Audubon magazine. Congressman John F. Lacey, at the urging of Audubon members, sponsored legislation that prohibits the illegal killing of birds and animals and the importation of non-native species.

1901: The Audubon Model Law is passed, protecting water birds from plume hunting.

1902: Guy Bradley is hired as first Audubon game warden.

1903: President Theodore Roosevelt creates the first National Wildlife Refuge, on Florida's Pelican Island.

1905: The National Association of Audubon Societies is incorporated in New York State. William Dutcher is named first President. Guy Bradley, one of the first Audubon wardens, is murdered by game poachers in Florida.

1910: New York State legislature enacts the Audubon Plumage Law, prohibiting the sale or possession of feathers from protected bird species.

1913–1918: Congress passes a landmark law placing all migratory birds under federal protection. Three years later President Woodrow Wilson re-signs the law to include an international treaty provision between the U.S. and Canada.

1914: Martha, the last living Passenger Pigeon, dies.

1918: The Migratory Bird Treaty Act is ratified.

1923–24: Audubon opens its first sanctuaries: Rainey Sanctuary in Louisiana and Theodore Roosevelt Sanctuary in Long Island.

1934: Roger Tory Peterson's field guide is published, popularizing birding like never before.

The Audubon Society maintains an office and display center at Joppa Flats that can be helpful to visitors.

1936: Audubon opens a nature camp on Hog Island, Maine.

1940: The National Association of Audubon Societies becomes the National Audubon Society.

1943: The Greenwich Audubon Center in Connecticut opens as Audubon's first nature center.

1945: Audubon magazine sounds the first alarm about the hazards of DDT. Audubon partners with the U.S. Fish and Wildlife Service on the Whooping Crane Project.

1953: Audubon adopts a flying Great Egret, one of the chief victims of turn-of-the-century plume hunters, as its symbol.

1954: Audubon buys the last great stand of bald cypress trees in Florida's Corkscrew Swamp to create the crown jewel of its sanctuary system.

1960: The Audubon Society begins documenting the decline of bird species, including bald eagles, attributing this to DDT.

1969: Audubon opens a public policy office in Washington, D.C.

1972: A campaign by the Environmental Defense Fund and the National Audubon Society ends in victory when the U.S. Environmental Protection Agency bans the use of the insecticide DDT.

1973: Endangered Species Act, considered the nation's toughest wildlife law, is passed, protecting hundreds of threatened and endangered species. Stephen Kress founds Project Puffin off the coast of Maine.

1980: The Alaska National Interest Lands Conservation Act is passed, protecting 79.5 million acres, including the Arctic National Wildlife Refuge.

1984: Audubon starts the popular new children's educational program and publication *Audubon Adventures*.

1987: Audubon biologists help capture the last wild California Condor, which is placed in a captive breeding program with other survivors.

1988: The first condor chick is born in captivity in California, raising new hope for the species' survival.

1994: The bald eagle is downlisted from endangered to threatened.

1998: Audubon holds its first-ever Great Backyard Bird Count: 14,000 people participate.

1999: Almost 50,000 participants take part in the 100th Christmas Bird Count, now the longest-running bird survey in the world.

2000: With Audubon at the forefront, President Bill Clinton authorizes the Everglades Protection and Restoration Act, committing $7.8 billion.

2002: Audubon opens its first urban Audubon Center, in Prospect Park, Brooklyn, New York; the center serves 50,000 visitors annually. The last free-flying California Condor is released back into the wild with more than 40 others.

2004: Audubon's science team releases the first "State of the Birds" report, the best data available since *Silent Spring* to document bird health and habitat.

2008: Toyota TogetherGreen, Audubon's most ambitious corporate partnership, begins transforming communities and bringing new diversity to conservation.

2010: Audubon signs a collaborative agreement with Birdlife International

2011: A multimillion-dollar strategic partnership between Audubon and Esri creates network-wide GIS mapping capability.

2014: Audubon releases its watershed climate report. Based on decades of data, Audubon scientists predict that, by 2080, 314 species will be threatened, endangered, or possibly extinct, due to habitat loss wrought by climate change.

13

The U.S. Fish and Wildlife Service Has Been a Leader on Plum Island

This essay on the history of the U.S. Fish and Wildlife Service appears on the organization's website.

The Fish and Wildlife Service programs are among the oldest in the world dedicated to natural resource conservation. One can trace its history back to 1871 and the U.S. Commission on Fish and Fisheries in the Department of Commerce and the Division of Economic Ornithology and Mammalogy in the Department of Agriculture.

Many prominent figures in the history of American wildlife conservation have been associated with what would become the Fish and Wildlife Service, including Spencer Fullerton Baird, first curator of the Smithsonian Institute, J. N. "Ding" Darling, originator of the Duck Stamp, and perhaps its most famous employee, *Silent Spring* author Rachel Carson.

The U.S. Fish and Wildlife Service is the federal government agency dedicated to the conservation, protection, and enhancement of fish, wildlife, and plants, and their habitats. It is the only federal agency whose primary responsibility is the conservation and management of these important natural resources for the American public.

The service's origins date back to 1871 when Congress established the U.S. Fish Commission to study the decrease in the nation's food fishes and recommend ways to reverse that decline. Today, it is a diverse and largely decentralized organization, employing about 8,000 professionals working out of facilities across the country, including a headquarters office in Falls Church, Virginia, and eight regional offices representing the twelve unified interior regions.

The headquarters office has primary responsibility for policy formulation and budget allocation within major program areas, while the regional offices have primary responsibility for implementation of these policies and management of field operations.

The director, supported by two deputy directors, oversees national programs, managed by programmatic assistant directors and the service's regions, each overseen by a regional director.

On the road to Plum Island is the local headquarters of the Parker River National Wildlife Refuge.

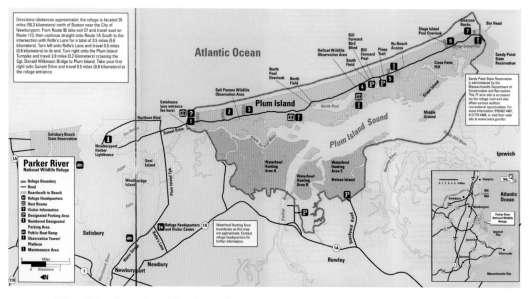

A map of Plum Island, produced by the Parker River National Wildlife Refuge.

The agency is responsible for implementing key environmental laws, such as the Endangered Species Act, Migratory Bird Treaty Act, Pittman-Robertson/Dingell-Johnson wildlife and sportfish restoration laws, Lacey Act, North American Wetlands Conservation Act, and Marine Mammal Protection Act. It offers an array of programs, activities, and offices that function to: protect and recover threatened and endangered species; monitor and manage migratory birds; restore nationally significant fisheries; enforce federal wildlife laws and regulate international wildlife trade; conserve and restore fish and wildlife habitat such as wetlands; manage and distribute over a billion dollars each year to states, territories and tribes for fish and wildlife conservation; and fulfill federal tribal trust responsibility.

Under the National Wildlife Refuge System Administration Act, it manages a network of 567 National Wildlife Refuges, with at least one refuge in each U.S. state and territory, and with more than 100 refuges close to major urban centers.

The Refuge System plays an essential role in providing outdoor recreation opportunities to the American public. In 2019, more than 59 million visitors went to refuges to hunt, fish, observe or photograph wildlife, or participate in environmental education or interpretation.

Also, the department promotes conservation for imperiled species through the administration of the Endangered Species Act, which has been successful in preventing the extinction of more than 99 percent of the species it protects. It is committed to the recovery of listed species and to returning management of those species to our state and tribal partners when they no longer require protections.

The Migratory Bird Program works to conserve birds and preserve traditional subsistence and outdoor recreational pursuits involving birds, as well as migratory bird management, cooperation with states, and environmental reviews. The program works with partners such as outdoor recreation and sporting groups, conservation organizations, tribes, and state wildlife agencies to conserve habitats needed to support these populations for future generations of Americans.

The Fish and Aquatic Conservation Program works with partners and the public to manage fish and other aquatic resources to achieve the goals of healthy, self-sustaining populations, and the conservation or restoration of their habitats. The National Fish Hatchery System provides fish to states and tribes, while also propagating and providing refugia for endangered aquatic species enabling us to fulfill our trust responsibilities and Tribal partnerships.

The International Affairs Program leads domestic and international efforts to protect, restore, and enhance the world's diverse wildlife and their habitats. FWS works to ensure that wildlife trade is both legal and sustainable to benefit the survival of species and domestic economies through the implementation of the Convention on International Trade in Endangered Species of Wild Fauna and Flora (CITES) and domestic wildlife laws. FWS also provides technical and financial assistance to partners to support innovative projects that address wildlife trafficking.

Its Office of Law Enforcement facilitates a multi-billion-dollar legal wildlife trade, while simultaneously interdicting illegal wildlife and wildlife products and investigating wildlife trafficking crimes. The Office of Law Enforcement provides critical work in the fight against wildlife trafficking and the successful prosecution of criminals who break Federal and international wildlife laws.

14

Rachel Carson, Environmentalist and Promoter of Plum Island

Rachel Carson is known for her book, *Silent Spring* (1962), but it is interesting to contemplate that she spent time at Plum Island. In 1947, she studied the barrier island and wrote a lengthy essay on it. It can be found in the next chapter.

The mid-1940s were a time of political strife on the island. The Audubon Society and its thousands of birdwatchers on the North Shore were trying to take possession of much of the island. Hunters and fishermen were concerned they would be shut out if the naturalists took over. Hunters wanted to shoot birds, not make their lives more comfortable.

A compromise was eventually developed. Today, the Parker River Wildlife Refuge on Plum Island spreads over almost 4,700 acres. The presence of this protected "wilderness" has meant that crowded residential neighborhoods on the northern end of Plum Island cannot pervade the southern portion.

Rachel Carson was a remarkable advocate. She was well educated, and in later years testified frequently in Washington about the need to preserve marshes and open space for wildlife. However, her views met significant opposition. In the early 1960s, she was often ridiculed by angry men annoyed that their outdoor activities were being challenged by scientists.

Lobbyist-scientists for corporations like DuPont, which made DDT, constantly criticized her work. But her research remains valuable documentation in the ongoing conservation effort.

Rachel Carson joins Stoneham philanthropist Annie H. Brown in being unsung heroes of Plum Island. Brown gave money for land. Carson wrote convincing essays on the value of preserving acreage for migratory birds. These two women were advocates for wildlife long before it became fashionable.

Regarding Rachel Carson, biographer William Souder wrote a book titled *On a Farther Shore: The Life and Legacy of Rachel Carson* (Crown Publishers, 2012). He referenced her tenure in Newburyport. He wrote:

> As the Merrimack River nears the coast it comes to a series of small islands in the main channel. Just below these, on the south shore, stands a town, uncommonly charming even by New England standards, called Newburyport.

Environmentalist Rachel Carson spent the autumn of 1947 studying the wildlife of Plum Island. (*Courtesy photo*)

Carson worked here in 1947. She was a writer with the Federal Wildlife Service, and she wrote a pamphlet titled *Parker River: A National Wildlife Refuge*. It argued that conservation could co-exist with duck hunting.

The '40s were a time of turmoil on Plum Island when it came to hunting. Hunters in Massachusetts were concerned that birdwatchers would take over Plum Island, leaving them without a source of game. But Carson said that all Americans had a stake in saving shoreland.

She argued for the existence of a wildlife refuge on Plum Island to help migrating birds to survive. The reason, she said, was that birds needed a refuge like Plum Island during migration.

Carson, who reportedly brought a whiskey flask with her when she traveled into the field on cold November days on Plum Island, wrote:

A striking fact about the Atlantic flyway—a fact that's dominates the conservation problem—is the extremely limited area of its winter range compared with the vast extent of its breeding grounds. The nest area extends from Greenland across much of northern Canada; the wintering grounds are confined in a narrow strip of coast marshes along the east coast of the U.S. A map of the flyway looks like a huge, distorted funnel with a long slender stem. Imagine that for one half of the year all the contents of the funnel have to be contained within the stem and you can understand the compression of birds within the range.

One of Rachel Carson's key
interests on the island was the
black duck.

Park rangers who hosted her were concerned that hunters might harm Carson, who essentially opposed the shooters' goal of more dead ducks. No encounters were reported. Carson did go on to write an informative essay. And she insisted that conservation would help hunters. She argued that though sportsmen could not shoot in the Refuge, they could shoot near it. If more birds gathered as this aviary "safe spot," hunters could still get their limit.

She loved black ducks. Carson wrote:

> As you drive out from the town to Plum Island ... You can see them bobbing in the harbor, small black forms riding the outgoing tide, bobbing like boats at anchor. Today there are a thousand. Tomorrow there may be five thousand; next week, as many more.

Today, Rachel Carson is considered one of this country's first effective environmentalists. She was also very brave.

After her book *Silent Spring* came out in 1962, she was criticized by scientists from corporations like DuPont that made pesticides such as DDT. She was often called to Washington to testify before Congress. The notion that chemical companies might take a financial loss by dropping products like DDT was unnerving to corporate America.

Through the early 1960s, she was battling cancer. To fight the pesticide industry as well as this debilitating condition demonstrated great mental and physical fortitude. She continued to testify throughout the illness. She died in 1964.

Carson remains one of the great pioneers of environmental studies, though her fame came after her death. Born in 1907 in rural western Pennsylvania, she graduated in 1929 from Pennsylvania Women's College, now Chatham University. She earned a master's degree in zoology at Johns Hopkins University in 1932. Carson did post-graduate work at the Marine Biological Laboratory at Woods Hole, Mass.

It should be remembered that there was not much of an "environmental movement" in the 1950s and '60s, so her publication of data designed to preserve wildlife was relatively new. In 1962, *Silent Spring* appeared. In 1969, the Cuyahoga River in Ohio caught fire, and Americans from around the country became angered at the level of pollution that existed in rivers, lakes, and oceans.

Carson's work in the 1950s and '60s, coupled with the outrage about filthy waterways, helped inspire an environmental movement that led to the creation of the U.S. Environmental Protection Agency (1970). The Clean Water Act was passed in 1972.

Though the EPA was created after her death, her federal salaried research position with the U.S. Fish and Wildlife Service had enabled her to have an income that enabled her research.

Earlier books that came in part from her research position included *Under the Sea-Wind* (1941), *The Sea Around Us* (1951), and *The Edge of the Sea* (1955).

A federal park in honor of Rachel Carson stretches along the coast of northern New England.

In the early '70s, Maine Sen. Edmund Muskie and others cobbled together bipartisan support to pass the Clean Water Act of 1972. President Richard Nixon vetoed the bill.

Yet the Clean Water Act passed over his veto. Billions of dollars in federal grants were directed to programs to clean rivers, streams, lakes, and oceans. The Merrimack River and Plum Island benefited, as did hundreds of other water resources. That would include lakes, rivers, wetlands and the oceans. Rachel Carson's testimony before Congressional panels in the 1960s is considered an important development on the way to the Clean Water Act of 1972.

In the 1940s, many birdwatchers urged federal officials to set aside land so that black ducks, shown here, and other birds could survive.

15

Parker River:
A National Wildlife Refuge

This essay on Plum Island was written for the U.S. Fish and Wildlife Service by Rachel Carson when she was an employee in 1947.

IF YOU TRAVEL MUCH in the wilder sections of our country, sooner or later you are likely to meet the sign of the flying goose-the emblem of the National Wildlife Refuges. You may meet it by the side of a road crossing miles of flat prairie in the Middle West, or in the hot deserts of the Southwest. You may meet it by some mountain lake, or as you push your boat through the winding salty creeks of a coastal marsh. Wherever you meet this sign, respect it. It means that the land behind the sign has been dedicated by the American people to preserving, for themselves and their children, as much of our native wildlife as can be retained along with our modern civilization.

Wild creatures, like men, must have a place to live. As civilization creates cities, builds highways, and drains marshes, it takes away, little by little, the land that is suitable for wildlife. And as their space for living dwindles, the wildlife populations themselves decline. Refuges resist this trend by saving some areas from encroachment, and by preserving in them, or restoring where necessary, the conditions that wild things need in order to live.

The Parker River National Wildlife Refuge is New England's most important contribution to the national effort to save the waterfowl of North America. Many million Americans have a direct stake in the success of this effort: the 2 million waterfowl hunters, the millions who find recreation and pleasure in observing and photographing the birds, and all those, whom there is no way of counting, who understand the value of preserving wildlife as part of America's natural heritage.

During the several generations in which the United States has been converted from a land preeminently wild and unsettled into an industrial and agricultural country, the waterfowl have been driven from most of the areas where they once lived. During the same span of years, we have seen the rise and decline of market gunning and the steady and continuing rise of hunting for sport. In this period there have been at least three major declines in the waterfowl population. From the first two, which reached their respective low points in 1915 and in the 1930s, there was a partial recovery. The third great decline began in 1944.

Canada Geese thrive in many parts of New England.

The downward sweep of such a cyclic decline—perhaps this, or the next, or the next—may reduce the flocks of wildlife refuge waterfowl to so low a point that there can be no recovery. To save the wild fowl, one of the most important things we can do is to reserve for their use areas which provide them with the marshes and ponds, the natural foods, and the sanctuary that they need in order to live in the midst of our civilization. Two hundred national waterfowl refuges scattered over the United States now provide these things. Whatever else waterfowl conservation demands, this is essential.

The Parker River lies some 30 miles north of Boston in the coastal marshes of Essex County, Massachusetts. The refuge was established late in 1942, but its active development to bring out its maximum usefulness had to be delayed until near the end of the war because of manpower and materials shortages.

However, in this brief time, its use by waterfowl has increased sharply. In the spring of 1944, about 2,000 waterfowl used the refuge. Two years later, the spring count was nearly 15,000. Regular patrons of the refuge include 19 species of ducks, of which the great majority are black ducks, and 1 species of goose, the Canada.

Greater snow and blue geese are reported casually. About 70 birds of other species make regular use of the refuge and many others occur as transients. The Essex County marshes are within the Atlantic flyway, which is one of four great geographic divisions into which the North American continent may be divided according to the ways of waterfowl. The term "flyway" as ornithologists use it today includes the breeding and wintering grounds and most of the migratory paths that connect them.

Birds have a hereditary attachment for one particular flyway and as a rule never transfer from one to another. A striking fact about the Atlantic flyway—a fact which dominates the conservation problem—is the extremely limited area of its winter range compared with the vast extent of its breeding grounds.

The nesting area extends from Greenland across much of northern Canada; the wintering grounds are confined to a narrow strip of coastal marshes along the east coast of the United States.

A map of the flyway looks like a huge, distorted funnel with a long slender stem. Imagine that for one-half of the year all the contents of the funnel have to be contained within the stem and you can understand the compression of birds within their winter range. This fact makes wildlife refuges especially important on the Atlantic flyway.

Parker River is the only Federal refuge operated principally for waterfowl on the northern part of the Atlantic flyway. It lies in the path of a great many of the ducks and geese that fly south in the fall from the eastern Canadian Provinces and from northern New England. Some of these birds follow a route roughly corresponding to the outlines of the seacoast; others fly overland from inland breeding grounds and make their first contact with the coast in the vicinity of Parker River.

These facts have in recent times been substantiated by bird banding. Recoveries of banded birds are demonstrating the pattern of migration. The general route of the waterfowl has been known for generations, however, and has been fully recorded in many publications by New England ornithologists. Dr. Charles Townsend pointed out that Essex County (site of Parker River) lay "in one of the great highways of bird migration."

Dr. John Phillips rated Plum Island worth a visit to see "all sorts of migrants." Edward Forbush, years ago, declared it "the most important region on our coast" in which to locate a bird sanctuary.

In the early 1930s the Massachusetts Audubon Society acted upon this advice. It acquired some 1,600 acres in the central portion of the island and converted it into a sanctuary. This former Audubon Society sanctuary is now part of the National Wildlife Refuge.

Parker River is a link in the chain of refuges established at carefully chosen intervals on the Atlantic flyway, so that the migrating waterfowl may find sanctuary and food at least every few hundred miles of their journey within the United States. Of the coastal refuges of the flyway, the migrations of the bird link Parker River toward the north with Moosehorn, near Calais, Maine, and toward the south with Brigantine on the ocean coast of New Jersey, and Bombay Hook, almost directly west on the shores of Delaware Bay.

Then come Blackwater in Maryland; Chincoteague and Back Bay, Virginia; Pea Island and Mattamuskeet in North Carolina; Cape Romain in South Carolina; and Savannah on the border between South Carolina and Georgia.

Waterfowl sanctuaries must be located in the kind of country that attracts birds, provides proper food for them, gives them suitable places to rest before making the next hop on the long migratory flight. Parker River is this kind of country.

Plum Island, the heart of the refuge, is a long, narrow, coastal island. It begins where the Merrimack pours its waters into the Atlantic and ends to the south at Ipswich Bay. To get a panoramic view of Plum Island, climb one of the highest sand dunes. The dune topped by the Army Observation Tower is one of the best lookout points. As your eyes range from east to west, you see five totally different kinds of country as the birds would

Birdwatchers have argued for years that setting aside wetlands in areas like Plum Island will result in more waterfowl.

Shorebirds make Plum Island one of the leading birding destinations in the country.

classify it, five different zones of life each containing a different community of animal life.

These regions are the ocean beach, the dunes, the thickets, the salt meadows, and the tidal flats of the salt marsh creeks. Eastward from our observation point is the immensity of the Atlantic, nothing but water between you and Spain. Outlined by the white surf lines, a sandy beach runs the length of the island. The large grains of the Plum Island sand do not pack to a hard surface; for this reason, driving on the beach is difficult and should be indulged in only by those who know local conditions and are experienced in driving on sand.

On the landward edge of the beach, where the beachgrass Ammophila and the silvery-leaved dusty-miller have begun to anchor the shifting grains, the dunes begin. Their contours are often steep, and as you look southward over the expanse of sand hills you see that the dune zone is pitted with many sandy depressions like bomb craters, their conical sides almost bare of plant growth. Except in these places, the dunes are widely covered with a low, sage-green carpet of the plant Hudsonia, helping to hold the shifting sand and prevent the sea beach from engulfing the land.

A scattered growth of bayberry and poison-ivy begins midway across the dunes, gradually becomes denser and merges with the thickets that run down the center of the island. Cranberries grow abundantly in the low, wet places among the sand hills. The shrubs, vines, and small trees that form the zone of thickets are the home of the small land birds and give excellent cover and food for the pheasants.

Probably the island supports from 60 to 75 pheasants—the only upland game bird on the island. Deer find good browsing here, as well as places of concealment from the casual eye. Most abundant plants are wild rose, sumac, beach plum, bayberry, black alder, choke cherry, pitch pine, aspen, and the ever-present green brier.

Lying to the west, almost like another vast green sea, are the salt meadows. The winding Plum Island River, the lower reaches of the Parker, and all their small, meandering tributaries traverse the marshes with an intricate series of open-water canals. Scattered ponds or potholes bring down the migrating wildfowl to feed on the water plants that grow in them.

Look out over the marshes when the tide is high, and you see nothing but grass and water. But look again when the tide is on the ebb, and you will see that every creek has a border of black mud. At dead low tide the small creeks are completely drained; even the large ones have only a central channel in the midst of a great expanse of mud. These are the clam flats, home of the soft-shell clam.

The conservation program at Parker River is designed to restore and if possible, to increase the black duck population. The refuge has many other uses and many values, but these are secondary to its principal purpose. There is a logical reason for concentrating on the black duck. Of all waterfowl, no other is so typical of New England as this species. From Cape Cod north, it is the only surface-feeding duck present in large enough numbers to maintain hunting for any considerable number of gunners.

A serious reduction in the population of black ducks would mean the end of waterfowl hunting for the majority of the New England sportsmen. For many years, even in the famous "duck depression" of the 1930s, the black duck held its own better than the ducks that breed in the central prairies of Canada and northern United States, then stricken by drought.

Birdwatchers love encountering a snowy owl, and here is a remarkable photo taken at Plum Island. (*Dan Graovac photo*)

However, it did not respond so dramatically to restorative efforts as some other species. In recent years there have been danger signals. Massachusetts observers, including outstanding ornithologists of the region, began as early as 1943 to report a scarcity of black ducks. Again in 1944 the blacks were reported as having fallen off sharply; in 1945 the flight was described as a "complete failure;" in 1946 observers warned that the species was "notably down in numbers."

We need to know more about the biology of this species to understand fully what has happened to the black duck, normally a hardy and adaptable species, and once so abundant. But this much we know: Many areas in northeastern United States where black ducks once nested have been drained out of existence as breeding grounds. Innumerable potholes have been filled for suburban residential sites and for industrial use.

Black ducks are to be found at Parker River any month of the year, but in September and October, almost more than any other time, you begin to get the feel of real black duck country as you tramp through the salt marshes of Plum Island. After the lull of midsummer, when only a few ducks are to be found here, migrants are coming in from the north. The great Joppa Flats in Newburyport Harbor are an early rallying point for them as they swing down from Labrador, Nova Scotia, Ontario, Maine, or wherever they may have summered. As you drive out from the town to Plum Island, you can see them gathering in the harbor, small black forms riding the outgoing tide, bobbing like boats at anchor. Today perhaps there are a thousand. Tomorrow morning there may be five thousand, next week as many more.

Soon the ducks spread out into the nearby marshes. Seeds of the salt-meadow plants—arrowgrass, bulrushes, tidemarsh waterhemp, pondweeds—are choice duck foods, abundant in the marshes through which Parker River and half a dozen other

We were all little once, like this tiny plover. (*Dan Graovac photo*)

creeks and small rivers cut their paths to the sea. As the late summer days pass and autumn comes, many ducks gather in the marsh potholes south of the Cross farm. In the days when there was no refuge here, the first roar of guns at the opening of the hunting season would send the ducks out to sea. They were safe there from the barrage of lead.

But the open ocean provides little or no food for a black duck and for that reason it was a poor sanctuary. Now the onset of the hunting season tends to concentrate the ducks in the refuge, where experience has quickly taught them, they can find both safety and food. Hunters now find better shooting in the marshes on the mainland than before the refuge was established, and the good hunting lasts longer because the ducks are not driven immediately from the vicinity.

So, by a seeming paradox, the refuge has improved hunting even while it has helped conserve the ducks. The tide of black duck migration runs strong through October and November. By December most of the migrants have passed through to the south.

These ducks, as we know from the returns of banded birds, winter in southern New England, on the New Jersey coast, in Chesapeake and Delaware Rays, some even as far south as Georgia. But some of the blacks stay at Parker River over winter, defying blizzards, freezing marshes, ice, and snow. The records of the area report wintering black ducks, suggesting that this is a deep seated, instinctive behavior.

In a severe winter, duck food is scarce on the northern Massachusetts coast. The coastal marshes often lie under a deep covering of snow and ice. As the highest tides break up the ice, the ducks find some food on the top of the marsh and along the creek banks. At low tide they search the patches of open water. When the cold is at its bitterest, they subsist on mussels, snails, scuds, minnows—all the varied life of the salt marshes.

They grow thin, sometimes losing as much as a pound—a third or more of their total weight over winter. Some actually die of starvation. By the time the ice has left the salt marshes, usually in March, many of the ducks are paired off. You can see them on the high tides in every little gut and puddle. As fast as freshwater areas open up, blacks appear on them. As the season advances, the paired birds go north to the nesting grounds in loosely organized flocks. A few pairs stay in the vicinity. About mid-April the female begins to search the thickets about the marsh edges for a likely nesting site. She collects grass stems and in a dense patch of meadowsweet or bayberry she fashions a nest, carefully lining it with down.

The first broods of ducklings appear at Parker River about May 15. The males do not take part in incubation; during the nesting season they gather in bachelor clubs, congregating in ponds and open water.

Barring molestation by enemies or other disaster, each nest produces a brood of about 10 ducklings. The youngsters take to the water almost immediately. In company with their mother, they feed in shallow water, sheltered by overhanging grasses and water plants. As the season advances, enemies thin the broods of young ducks until, by late summer, the average family is 3 or 4.

By August the young ducks have exchanged their down for feathers, have tested them in flight, and now spend much time a-wing. Another month and they are ready, when the big migrations pass over Parker River, to take their place in the southward flights of the waterfowl.

Canada Geese move in their long wavering Vs over the coastal marshes of Essex County, spring and fall. Only a few years ago, flocks of several thousands of these magnificent waterfowl visited Newburyport Harbor during March. Fall flights along

Canada Geese are common and graceful.

the northeastern coast are usually somewhat smaller than the spring flights. Reports of the refuge managers at Parker River give a good idea of the habits of the Canadas while in this area.

In 1943, for example, the manager reported that a few Canada geese were present all through the winter, and that migrants from the south appeared by the time most of the ice was out of the marshes and tidal areas. Many of the geese congregated in the lower Merrimack around Woodbridge Island; others worked down to Plum Island. On the flood tides they came high into the marshes to rest or eat the new shoots of the tall marsh grass. As soon as the freshwater areas lost their ice, the geese tended to separate into smaller flocks and move to small outlying ponds, where they could be seen tipping up and feeding. On the refuge, several patches of land have now been sown to rye as a source of food for migrating geese.

The blue-winged teal, among other waterfowl transients, should benefit from freshwater dykes on the marshes at Parker River. This small and beautiful duck formerly nested in all the middle and northern states east of the Rocky Mountains. But gradually it was driven from the Eastern States as a breeding bird. Even in the prairie regions of northern United States and Canada, encroaching agriculture menaced it and widespread drought destroyed its broods.

Ducks of several kinds—especially the scaups, scoters, goldeneye, bufflehead, old squaw, and mergansers—endure the rigorous winter climate of the northern Massachusetts coast.

Along with the black duck and the scaup, the goldeneye is part of the dominant waterfowl population during the season when cold, storms, and ice have driven all less hardy fowl to the south. The goldeneyes first appear in the refuge waters about the middle of November. In recent years, Christmas census has reported one to two thousand goldeneyes off Plum Island in the surf. Then there are always a few hundred buffleheads, old squaws, and scoters that linger over winter. They come during November. The scoters like the rock jetties near Bar Head, where they may often be seen diving near the rocks, even when heavy seas are rolling. The buffleheads and old squaws mingle with them.

Improving the land for wildlife means, first, increasing the natural food supplies, providing more cover, adjusting the water levels, improving conditions for breeding. Within a wildlife refuge, if it is a successful one, there is a much heavier concentration of birds and animals than in the surrounding country. Seasonally, as the migrations pass, the facilities of a refuge often are taxed to provide for the large number of transients that seek accommodations.

To provide enough food, water, cover, and nesting areas for its patrons, a wildlife refuge must be a small, separate world in which all these things exist in greater abundance than in the world outside-a wildlife Utopia. To bring about these ideal conditions is the aim of refuge management.

From August or early September until the winter freeze-up of the marshes, the seeds of these plants are easily available and so furnish food for the ducks during the fall migration. To increase the production of food plants, a system of shallow flowages will be created in the marshes by impounding the water behind dikes. From small, experimental beginnings, these bodies of fresh or brackish water, about a foot and a half deep, will eventually become an important part of the Parker River refuge.

Plum Island offers natural settings at dawn and at night. (*Dan Graovac photo*)

To the waterfowl hunter, a wildlife refuge is an investment. Let us say that 5,000 acres of marsh are "invested" in waterfowl conservation by converting them into a refuge. It is true that this area is withdrawn from hunting, just as money you invest in stocks is no longer in your pocket to spend. In a few years, however, the refuge investment begins to pay the sportsmen dividends.

Almost immediately, hunting in areas near the refuge improves. The birds are held in the area longer; the hunting season, as a result, is lengthened. Birds moving in and out of the refuge area provide hunting in nearby marshes. This is common experience. It is acknowledged by many Massachusetts gunners at Parker River. Black ducks that formerly were frightened out to sea by the first shots of the hunting season now stay in and about the refuge.

The most substantial dividends on the refuge investment come after a period of 5 to 10 years has passed. Then it will be found that waterfowl use has increased several hundred percent or more. Such increases at well-established Federal refuges are a matter of record. The Bombay Hook Refuge in Delaware is a good example. Here the number of waterfowl using the area has increased more than 400 percent since the refuge was established in 1937.

Official reports show that it was used by 30,000 wildfowl in the fall of 1937, by 60,000 in 1942, and by 137,000 in 1945. When this happens, the sportsman understands the wisdom of the investment he and his fellow citizens have made. Instead of interfering with his sport, the refuge has increased it and made its future more secure.

The season for harvesting both fruits ends with the first hard frosts. Salt-marsh hay is another product of the extensive salt meadows of the refuge. Neighboring farmers find it profitable to harvest the hay, which they use as bedding and to some extent as food for their stock. An acre of salt meadow yields nearly a ton of hay per year.

The refuge manager issues permits for cutting, giving preference to former owners of the land. From the standpoint of wildlife conservation, cutting the grass on the meadows has great value. Shore birds flock into these cut-over areas. Among the short stubble all the small food animals of the marshes are more easily found and captured. Cutting the hay on the salt meadows just before or during the fall shore bird migration greatly increases the natural food supply for these birds at a time when they particularly need it.

Some of the scarcer east coast shore birds can be seen feeding on these hay meadows in August and September. The black-bellied plover is especially attracted to them. Although Plum Island once contained summer camps and cottages, most of these properties had lapsed into an uninhabitable state of decay before the Government bought the property for a wildlife refuge. Access to all but the northern end of the island is extremely difficult.

The road that makes its tortuous way between the dunes and the marshes is often impassable except to jeeps or command cars. Fresh water is at a minimum everywhere, nonexistent in many places. Most property owners on Plum Island were glad to sell to the Government. Those who wished to remain did so under special arrangement.

For the bird clubs of eastern Massachusetts, Parker River has in irresistible attraction. This attraction is based on a very practical reason: A greater variety of birds can be seen here than almost anywhere else in the State.

Essex County, site of the refuge, has records of 357 different species. To give some meaning to this figure, consider one of the best-known birding grounds in eastern United States, Cape May County in New Jersey, where the record is 318. The majority of the birds of Essex County may be observed in the coastal sections which include Parker River. Scarcely a week passes at the refuge without a visit from some bird club, nature study group, or scout troop. Some of the visitors are serious students of bird life; some are having their first introduction to the rewarding hobby of amateur bird study.

Still others, without direct interest in the birds themselves, find in this outdoor recreation a welcome and refreshing release from the tensions of modern life. Observant photographers find many opportunities on the refuge for close-ups of the native birds. Little parties of sandpipers run along the beach, unsuspicious and unafraid. The richly colored killdeers along the road deserve color photography. Where clam shells, not long out of the shucking houses, have been dumped on the road, herring gulls hover above them in a cloud, so intent on picking the fragments of meat from the shells that they scarcely notice the approach of people. In the meadows and on the mud flats the shore birds can be approached rather closely.

One can always see curlews in the fall, standing like tall brown sentinels in the marsh; yellowlegs are a common sight as they wade the salt pools or chase minnows over a barely flooded flat. In September 1946 a rare species of shore bird appeared on Plum Island, the Hudsonian godwit. Look carefully out over the marshes and you are sure to be rewarded with some sort of heron, standing motionless in the manner of herons—a good camera shot if you have a telescopic lens.

There may be an American egret, a great blue heron, more rarely a bittern. Where the marsh hay is harvested, the stakes driven into the marsh to form the "straddles" for the haystacks are favorite roosting places of the black-crowned night herons. Seen in early morning sunlight, their white breasts make them conspicuous for long distances. Plum Island, Joppa Flats, and Plum Island breakwater seem to attract more than their share of rare species, and the hope of surprising an ornithological rarity gives zest to often repeated visits. When the snowy owls periodically invade New England, birders visit Plum Island with reasonable assurance of finding one or more of these spectacular birds perched atop a salt haystack.

A few years ago, visitors came from places many miles distant to see the rare western grebe. At another time, a flock of 82 Lapland longspurs fed on the Plum Island meadows—probably the largest flock ever seen in the state. The first king eiders recorded for Essex County were seen off Plum Island.

The blue goose and the greater snow goose, both considered rare transients, are occasionally seen on the refuge, the latter with increasing frequency. Birding on the Joppa Flats or about the break- water at the northern tip of the island may yield such rare fowl as the European wigeon.

Botanists find many interesting plants among the dunes, thickets, and marshes. A fine record of the wildflowers, fruits, and berries of seaside New England can be made by any photographer who will visit the refuge at intervals with color film in his camera.

The Parker River National Wildlife Refuge covers almost 4,700 acres.

16

Federal Duck Stamp Has Helped Wildlife

The Federal Duck Stamp program has been a valuable tool for raising money for wildlife conservation since 1934. This excerpt comes from federal government documents.

Formally known as the Migratory Bird Hunting and Conservation Stamp, it features an adhesive stamp issued by the United States federal government that must be purchased prior to hunting for migratory waterfowl such as ducks and geese.

It is also used to gain entrance to National Wildlife Refuges that normally charge for admission. It is widely seen as a collectable and a means to raise funds for wetland conservation with 98 percent of the proceeds of each sale going to the Migratory Bird Conservation Fund.

President Herbert Hoover signed the Migratory Bird Conservation Act in 1929 to authorize the acquisition and preservation of wetlands as waterfowl habitat. The law, however, did not provide a permanent source of money to buy and preserve the wetlands. On March 16, 1934, Congress passed, and President Roosevelt signed, the Migratory Bird Hunting Stamp Act, popularly known as the Duck Stamp Act. Duck stamps are now issued by the United States government and all state governments.

The issuing authorities within the various governments that release duck stamps are usually conservation and wildlife departments. These programs must be created by some form of legislation for the resulting stamps to be accepted as a valid governmental issue. Labels featuring ducks also are issued by various special interest groups, such as Ducks Unlimited and the National Fish and Wildlife Foundation.

Their issues are referred to as "society stamps." These items technically are not duck stamps because the fee structure and disposition of funds are not legislated. However, society stamps are very collectible and often appreciated. Funds raised by these organizations are also used for waterfowl and conservation efforts. Valid organizations and societies of this type perform a major service to conservation by their donations and efforts, and they merit public support.

Duck stamps are issued once a year. In most states, hunters are required to purchase both a federal and state stamp before hunting waterfowl. Waterfowl hunting seasons

Kayaking is one form of transportation on Plum Island, and there are several sites from which visitors can launch. (*Courtesy photo*)

vary, but most begin in September or October, so naturally, stamps are needed prior to opening day of the hunting season. Currently, the federal stamp and more than half of the state stamps are issued by July. Many are issued on the first day of the new year, and a few at the last minute in September or early October.

Most state conservation stamps have a face value of $5. New Hampshire has the lowest price at $4. Louisiana non-resident is the highest at $25. Funds generated from state stamps are designated for wetlands restoration and preservation, much like the federal funds, but with a more localized purpose. Most state agencies sell their stamps at face value. However, some also charge a premium to collectors buying single stamps, to help cover overhead costs.

The federal stamp is presently issued in panes of 20 stamps. Originally, the stamps were issued in panes of 28, but because of a change in the printing method (and to make stamps easier to count) a 30-stamp format was adopted in 1959. In 2000, the format was again changed to the present sheet of 20. Beginning in 1998, a single self-adhesive stamp was issued. This stamp and surrounding backing is approximately the size of a dollar bill. Most states and foreign governments follow the federal format. Many states issue a 10-stamp pane for ease of handling and mailing to field offices.

Currently, about 10 states issue two types of stamps, one for collectors and another for hunter use. Collector stamps are usually in panes of 10 or 30 without tabs. Hunter type stamps are usually issued in panes of five or 10, many with tabs attached. Hunters use the tabs to list their name, address, age and other data. Some states use only serial numbers to designate their hunter type stamp. State stamps are therefore referred to as either collector stamps or hunter type stamps. Most dealers will distinguish between these types on their price lists. Separate albums exist for both types and are available from most dealers.

Plate blocks or control number blocks are designations given to a block of stamps, usually four, with a plate or control number present on the selvage. Such a block is usually located in one or all four corners of a pane. Federal stamps prior to 1959 plus the 1964 issue are collected in blocks of six and must have the selvage on two sides. The Federal Junior Duck Stamp Program is a non-profit program sponsored by the Federal Government and designed to promote interest in conservation and wetlands preservation among students in grades K-12. The program includes a conservation and education curriculum that helps students of all ages. It focuses on wildlife conservation and management, wildlife art and philately. All proceeds from sales support conservation education.

Governor's Editions have been issued by several state agencies as a means of raising additional income. These stamps are printed in small quantities, fewer than 1,000. They have a face value of approximately $50 and are imprinted with the name of the state governor. Governors also hand-sign a limited number of stamps. These are usually available at a premium, generally twice the price of normal singles. Hand-signed or autographed stamps are issued in very small quantities and are scarce to rare. Governor's Editions are valid for hunting by all issuing states thus far. Obviously, none would be used for the purpose, however, as it would destroy the mint condition and lower the value of the stamp.

A heavy buoy was driven on shore during a blustery storm. (*Dan Gravoac photo*)

Artist signed stamps are mint examples of duck stamps autographed by the artist responsible for the artwork on the stamp. Such stamps are rapidly gaining popularity with collectors, and most can be purchased for a small premium over mint examples. Early federal stamps are particularly valuable and difficult to acquire. Signed stamps by artists now deceased also command a substantial premium. Remarqued stamps are quickly gaining in popularity with a worldwide audience. Original art on the actual stamp is seen as adding a spectacular flair to collections, making each stamp unique. These are very special, one-of-kind stamps on which an artist has personally drawn or painted a dog, decoy, lighthouse and/or duck.

The artwork is obtained by commissioning the artist for their work, and generally the stamps take time to complete. All are either signed or initialed by the artist. Stamps of deceased artists will bear a remarque by a living federal artist, as a "tribute" to the artist and their work.

Printed text stamps are another popular collectible. Generally, these preceded the later pictorial issues. The term is applied to stamps required for duck hunting that contain only writing but no waterfowl illustration. Certain American Indian reservations and tribes also issue waterfowl hunting stamps. The stamps of these sovereign Indian nations allow holders to hunt on that reservation when a federal stamp is also purchased. Reservation stamps are becoming increasingly popular with collectors as more people discover their existence.

While most collectors prefer to collect mint condition duck stamps, many others prefer collecting stamps on license, autographed stamps, plate blocks, stamps signed by hunters, art prints, souvenir cards, first day covers, or a combination.

Preserving the mint condition of a stamp is crucial for determining value. A perfectly centered stamp will usually sell for a substantial premium over one with normal centering. Very fine (VF) is the norm in stamp collecting, and is the condition priced by Scott Catalog.

The first Federal Duck Stamp, designed by Jay, "Ding" Darling in 1934 at President Franklin D. Roosevelt's request, depicts two mallards about to land on a marsh pond. In subsequent years, other noted wildlife artists were asked to submit designs. The first contest in 1949 was open to any U.S. artist who wished to enter. Sixty-five artists submitted 88 design entries that first year. The number of entries rose to 2,099 in 1981.

A panel of noted art, waterfowl, and philatelic authorities is appointed by the Secretary of the Interior to judge each competition. Winners receive no compensation for their work, other than a pane of stamps carrying their design. Winning artists may sell prints of their designs, which are sought after by hunters, conservationists, and art collectors.

The U.S. Fish and Wildlife Service mails contest regulations to interested artists each spring. Artists may choose their own medium and designs may be in black-and-white or full color and must measure 10 inches wide by 7 inches high.

17

Naturalist Mark Garland Offers Advice on Birdwatching

The following excerpt originated in Mark Garland's pamphlet *Birds of the New England Coast*. It was published by Earth, Wind and Water LLC in Wilton, N.H. (2016).

Use binoculars to see birds better. It takes practice to use binoculars quickly and skillfully.

Observe a bird carefully before using referring to a guide. Note basic color, length, shape, and color of bill, leg length and color, and behavior. Birds often disappear while you are checking.

Birding is often best early in the morning. Tides are important. Mudflats are most extensive at low tide, but higher tides often concentrate birds in a smaller area.

Utilize local nature center or refuge visitor centers. Compare notes with all birders you meet in the field

Observe birds from a distance so you don't make them alter their behavior. Shut car doors quietly. Speak softly, even if you see a rare bird for the first time.

Birds are along the New England coast all year long. Migration season peaks from March through May, and from August through October. Summer is when birds are nesting and raising young. A surprising number of birds spend winter along the coast.

18

Plum Island Took Bronze
for "Hottest" Birding Site

Here is a short story I wrote for *The Daily News* in Newburyport several years ago. It puts into context that Plum Island is "one of the most popular birding sites" in the country.

Birding is not known as a competitive sport, and yet a national birding service has ranked Plum Island as the third "hottest" birding site in the nation.

A list of the largest number of birds reported is kept by an online site called eBird to which birders report sightings. Launched in 2002 by the Cornell Lab of Ornithology and National Audubon Society, eBird provides basic information on bird abundance and distribution.

Organizers say that eBird's goal is "to maximize the utility and accessibility of the vast numbers of bird observations made each year by recreational and professional bird watchers." In May 2015, participants reported more than 9.5 million bird observations across the world, according to eBird's website.

In a recent assessment, Cape May Point in New Jersey ranked No. 1 with 369 species sighted (over a period of time). Aransas, in Austwell, Texas, ranked No. 2 with 366 and Plum Island was third with 365.

Members of the local branch of Mass Audubon on Plum Island Turnpike appear interested in the statistics but indicated they will not be launching a campaign to overcome Cape May Point.

"The list is interesting as citizen science, but we have no plans to try to lead the list," said David Larson, science and education coordinator at the Joppa Flats Education Center at the time. "Most of us think Plum Island is a great place to see birds, but we're not into the rah-rah stuff of competition."

The eBird list came to light recently when a birder named Curt Morgan, of Albany, N.Y., wrote to managers at Joppa to point out that Joppa is currently in third place. Morgan suggested that with effort and a plan, it could move up to first.

"I have noticed that Plum Island/Parker River National Wildlife Refuge has risen to be in the top three hot spots for birding in America. I enjoy a good contest as I am sure

Photographers flock to Plum Island, and so motorists must be careful. (*Bryan Eaton photo*)

you do," said Morgan, a frequent visitor, in an email to the Audubon officials at Joppa.

He suggested that Plum Island (Audubon) and the National Wildlife Refuge (a separate listing) work together, and perhaps the numbers would increase. "Plum Island could become the 'hottest hot spot' for birding in America, and what a great advertising that would make for Mass Audubon."

eBird documents the presence or absence of species, as well as bird abundance through checklist data. Its web-interface has inspired tens of thousands of participants to submit their observations or view results via interactive queries into the eBird database.

Other top birding "hot spots" include Bosque del Apache (Texas), Laguna Atascosa (Texas), Sandy Hook (New Jersey), and South Padre Island (Texas), according to eBird's top 10.

19

The Preservation of the Popular Piping Plover

This essay was produced by the U.S. Fish and Wildlife Service. Concern for plovers' welfare means that people sometimes cannot use the beaches at Plum Island.

The Atlantic Coast piping plovers are small, stocky, sandy-colored birds. Piping plovers resemble sandpipers. Adult plovers have yellow-orange legs, a black band across the forehead from eye to eye, and a black ring around the base of the neck. Plover chicks have been likened to tiny wind-up toys or cotton balls with legs. Like their parents, they run in short starts and stops. When still, adults and chicks blend into the pale background of open, sandy habitat on outer beaches where they feed and nest. The bird's name derives from its call - plaintive bell-like whistles often heard before the birds are seen.

Piping plovers were common along the Atlantic coast during much of the 19th century, but commercial hunting for feathers to decorate hats nearly wiped them out. Following passage of the Migratory Bird Treaty Act in 1918, plovers recovered to a 20th century peak in the 1940s. Increased development and beach recreation after World War II caused the population decline that led to Endangered Species Act protection in 1986. Intensive protection has helped the population more than double in the last 20 years, but the most recent surveys place the Atlantic population at fewer than 2,000 pairs.

Atlantic Coast piping plovers breed on coastal beaches from Newfoundland and southeastern Quebec to North Carolina. After they establish nesting territories and conduct courtship rituals beginning in late March or early April, pairs form shallow depressions—nests—in the sand on the high beach close to the dunes.

They sometimes line nests with small stones or fragments of shell. Plovers typically lay four eggs that hatch in about 25 days. The downy chicks are soon able to follow their parents in foraging for the marine worms, crustaceans and insects that they pluck from the sand and eat. Both the eggs and piping plover chicks blend into the beach so thoroughly that they are almost impossible to see.

When predators or intruders come close, the chicks squat motionless on the sand while the parents attempt to attract the attention of the intruders, often by feigning a broken wing. Surviving chicks are able to fly in about 30 days. Storm tides, predators or intruding humans sometimes disrupt nests before the eggs hatch. When this happens, the plovers often lay another clutch of eggs. Chicks hatched from these late-nesting efforts may not fly until late August. Piping plovers often gather in groups on undisturbed beaches before their southward migration. By mid-September, both adult and young plovers have departed for their wintering areas. These birds winter on the Atlantic coast from North Carolina south to Florida, along the Gulf coast, and in the Bahamas and West Indies.

The piping plover is designated as threatened along the Atlantic coast, which means that the population would become endangered and face possible extinction without Endangered Species Act protection. Recovery efforts include conserving breeding and wintering habitat, and protecting breeding birds, eggs, and chicks from predators and from disturbance and death caused by human activities.

Other rare species that inhabit the beach ecosystem, including the endangered roseate tern, the threatened northeastern beach tiger beetle, the threatened seabeach amaranth, least terns, common terns, black skimmers and Wilson's plovers, benefit from piping plover protection.

Many visitors to Plum Island between April and July are disappointed that they can't roam through much of the dunes. Refuge managers say, "We keep people out because so plovers can mate. We are a refuge, not a park."

The plover is a protected citizen of Plum Island.

20

Osprey:
Spring Signals Return of a Bird That Can Really Fish

This essay was written by Matt Poole, PI Wildlife Refuge visitor services manager, 2019.

When it comes to leading a behind-the-scenes tour at either Parker River or Great Bay NWR in New Hampshire during the spring and summer months, there is generally a no more reliable watchable wildlife opportunity than that provided by the osprey (*Pandion haliaetus*).

Tour participants are awed at the size and beauty of these large raptors, known to some as "fish hawks." Osprey nests at both refuges provide a unique opportunity to witness the breeding and feeding behavior of these fascinating birds.

Like so many other avian species impacted by the pesticide DDT, osprey numbers plummeted between the 1940s and late 1960s. In the early 1940s, between New York City and Boston, biologists had counted approximately 1000 osprey nests. By 1969, that number had dropped to 150. DDT caused eggshell thinning to the point that eggs would crush under the weight of the incubating parent. After the U.S. Government outlawed DDT in 1972, osprey numbers gradually rebounded, along with other DDT-affected species. Osprey are easy to identify. They are 22.5 to 25" long and have a 4.5–6' wingspan. Like many raptor species, the female is generally larger than the male.

White below and dark brown above, ospreys have a dark mask across the side of the head. The adult osprey has yellow eyes. Osprey primarily eat fish and capture their prey by diving into the open water, feet first, and grabbing them with their strong talons. An osprey can reach speeds up to 80 miles per hour in a dive, hitting the water with such an impact that its entire body dips below the water's surface! An osprey typically carries its catch through the air with the fish facing forward. In April, osprey return from wintering grounds located from the southern U.S. to northern coastal Mexico to northern South America. They nest along the coast, near large lakes and, increasingly, along major rivers.

Their nests, comprised primarily of sticks, are built on snags (standing dead trees), utility poles, cliffs rock faces, buoys and other navigational aids, and increasingly, on human-provided nest platforms. Ospreys mate for life. If one of the partners dies or

A popular bird throughout New England is the osprey. (*PBS photo*)

The nesting of ospreys has been well-documented. (*PBS photo*)

disappears for some other reason, the lone bird will often find a new mate. The average lifespan for an osprey in the wild is 7–10 years, though some birds can live 20 years or more. Typically, a clutch of one to four eggs appears in the nest in April or May. The average clutch size is three.

The female incubates the eggs for about 30 days, after which the young hatch over a five-to-six-day period. The male's role during incubation is to provide food and help protect the nest from predators. Osprey young fledge (or begin to fly) after about eight weeks. Immature osprey stay with their parents through late summer or early fall, after which they migrate, by themselves, to the wintering grounds. Two, or in some instances three years later, the young osprey migrate north to their natal breeding grounds for the first time. And, so, the cycle repeats. When it comes to visitor center exhibits, sometimes simple is best. Without a doubt, one of the most popular exhibits at the refuge visitor center during the warmer months is the television monitor that provides a live view of the "famous" osprey nest located on Hog Island in Maine.

That particular osprey "couple" has quite a following, including here at the Parker River National Wildlife Refuge.

After wintering along the Texas Gulf Coast and in Central America, ospreys begin returning to the Refuge in April. Very often, visitors hear these "fish hawks" before they see them. Ospreys have a very loud, whistled call. At Plum Island, watch for ospreys hovering over North and Bill Forward pools before they plunge feet first into the water after fish. From the observation tower at Hellcat, look to the southwest to see an osprey nesting platform in the distance. The return of red-winged blackbirds in early March, with their gurgling konk-a-ree [*sic.*] songs, marks the beginning of spring. Male blackbirds arrive a few weeks before the females.

For the males, the priority is to arrive early and establish the best breeding territories. The females linger farther south where the temperatures are a little warmer and food is more plentiful. For the females, arriving healthy is the imperative—they'll soon begin laying eggs and nurturing young.

21

Audubon Leaders Express Concern about Effect of Climate Change on Coastal Birds

The Massachusetts Audubon Society has been studying the effect of climate change on New England shorebirds for many years. Since 1896 when several Boston women came up with the idea of saving birds, the Audubon Society has been a leader in the protection of wildlife. The following are excerpts from the Audubon Society's State of the Birds Report of 2017, one of its most recent:

Creating a report to summarize the challenges our birds face as the climate changes takes us onto new ground. Our previous editions of State of the Birds analyzed data from the field to provide evidence of how our bird populations had changed over time. Those reports looked to the past, measured changes, and identified priority conservation actions.

This report is an effort to look into the future. We use new data to establish the preferred climates for various bird species (their "climate envelopes") and then use projections of the future climate to estimate how the distribution of each species' climate envelope will differ from its current climate envelope distribution by the year 2050. The changes in climate and sea level that we expect from a warming atmosphere include:

Increased average air temperature year-round
Longer warm seasons and shorter cold seasons
More precipitation will fall as rain, rather than snow
Increased frequency of large precipitation events
Longer growing seasons
Continued sea level rise, which is projected to increase an additional 2.4 to 7.4 feet by 2100 in Massachusetts.
More acidic oceans as carbon dioxide dissolves into the sea

The shifting climate is changing the fundamental way ecosystems work. A few items of highest conservation concern include the following:

Urgent action is required. Mass Audubon's previous research indicates 30 percent of our breeding birds are already declining and are in need of conservation action. Climate change will increase stress on many of those species, as well as additional species, and will do so in both predicted and unpredicted ways. Our climate change projections estimate that 43 percent of the breeding species we evaluated are Highly Vulnerable to climate change by the year 2050.

Fundamental processes are being disrupted. Warmer winters will alter marine food webs, affecting a wide range of interconnected fish and wildlife, including fish-eating birds. Increasing temperatures can shift the timing of important events, such as leaf and insect emergence. Those changes in phenology can cause declines in long-distance migrant birds as their arrival on their breeding grounds misses the periods of peak food abundance. Over 99 percent of the osprey's diet is fish.

Climate change adds stress to already stressed environments. Coastal nesting species are particularly at risk from this additional threat. Rising sea level will reduce nesting areas available for coastal nesting birds. Increasing frequency and intensity of storms will contribute to overwash of beaches and salt marsh flooding, adding stress to coastal birds. Increasing ocean acidification, caused by atmospheric carbon dioxide dissolving into the ocean, will cause large-scale changes to our shellfish and fish communities. Birds and wildlife that eat marine fish and shellfish will suffer from changes in the abundance of their prey.

One hundred forty-three (143) breeding species are evaluated in this report:

43 percent (61 species) are classified as Highly Vulnerable to climate change by the year 2050. An additional 15 percent (22 species) are classified as Likely Vulnerable.

42 percent (60 species) are classified as Least Vulnerable.

70 percent (7 species) of the salt marsh-nesting species are classified as Highly Vulnerable.

56 percent (9 species) of the coastal-nesting species are classified as Highly Vulnerable.

49 percent (30 species) of the forest breeding species are classified as Highly Vulnerable.

The Massachusetts state bird, the black-capped chickadee, is Highly Vulnerable, and the projected climate of eastern Massachusetts in 2050 could be unsuitable for the species. Other familiar birds that are Highly Vulnerable in the state, as well as in other continentwide analyses, are the yellow-bellied sapsucker, ruffed grouse, purple finch, magnolia warbler, and white-throated sparrow.

Urban- and suburban-nesting birds show the least vulnerability. For 77 percent (34 species), if climate is the only factor considered, projected climate changes contribute to stable or increasing trends by the year 2050.

Some species will have an expanding area of suitable climate by 2050. Many of these are urban and suburban nesting species, including the eastern kingbird, American robin, ruby-throated hummingbird, blue jay, great blue heron, and orchard oriole. Audubon officials say protecting our birds, and ourselves, from the most severe projected effects of climate change requires that we support our birds now and reduce our greenhouse gas emissions.

The gull is a common sight on New England beaches.

22

Plum Island Airport Has a Long and Colorful History

Plum Island Airport is not on Plum Island. It is on Plum Island Turnpike on the way to the island, but it has such an interesting history—to say nothing of its popular appeal—that it is included in this tome about Plum Island.

In some ways, the airport mirrors the city of Newburyport itself. Its history is fascinating despite being a very small operation.

Going back to the Age of Sail, Newburyport in the eighteenth and nineteenth centuries was not a large community. Yet in the eighteenth century, it was a major builder of vessels to support the American Revolution. In the nineteenth century, it was one of the most prosperous shipping communities in the young country.

The historian Samuel Eliot Morison stated that in the late eighteenth and early nineteenth centuries, there was no port in the country that built more ships than those constructed in the Merrimack River Valley, with Newburyport as the lead site.

In the twentieth century, some of the first flights in New England were staged in the Newburyport area. According to the museum at the airport and to Wikipedia, the first flying field in New England was on the dunes and marshes of Plum Island, about 1.5 miles east of the current airport. From there, from April to August 1910, Marblehead yacht designer W. Starling Burgess conducted a series of test flights with biplanes that he and Augustus Herring designed and built.

On February 28, 1910, the first airplane flight in New England took place when Herring—who had first tested gliders in 1895 with the "Father of Aviation," Octave Chanute, on the Lake Michigan dunes—took off from the frozen surface of Chebacco Lake in Hamilton, Mass., in a biplane he and Burgess built.

After the single flight, Burgess sold the plane and moved the operation to the marshes at Plum Island. He built a building and a wooden "runway" near where the dunes meet the marshes, about a mile south of the current entrance to the Parker River National Wildlife Refuge.

The test range included approximately the area bounded by the dunes, the Plum Island Turnpike, High Road, and the Parker River. The airplane, called the *Flying Fish*, first made three short flights on April 17. In May Burgess brought additional airplanes from Marblehead and built an additional building. Tests continued through the spring and summer of 1910 with longer and higher flights.

The earliest record of possible aviation scheduling at the current Plum Island Airport was in 1926, when the U.S. Army Air Service designated the field as an Emergency Landing Field. Sometime in 1926–1929, the new Civil Aviation Administration (now the FAA) installed a beacon tower at the Plum Island field as a primary navigation aid to mark the Boston–Portland air route. The base of the beacon tower can still be seen at the bend in the Plum Island Turnpike.

Commercial operation of the airfield began in August 1933 by Joseph Basso and W. F. Bartlett. In May 1937, John Polando began passenger service, airmail service, and pilot training flights at the airport. Polando was nationally famous as the holder of the long-distance flight record, together with a 1931 non-stop flight from New York to Istanbul.

With his partner, Warren Frothingham, Polando expanded airport facilities as business increased. In July 1937, a green light was added to the beacon, thus permitting all types of aircraft to land there. Three hangars, an office building, the asphalt runway, and a small building beside the beacon tower were built before World War II. The small building (the current airport office) was used for many years as a restaurant known as the Cockpit Café.

By 1940, the Civilian Pilot Training Program began operating at Plum Island. The CPT used the airport extensively until early 1942, when all civilian airports within 25 miles of the coast were ordered closed and flight training moved further inland. During World War II, the Coast Guard used the hangars, and a group of small airplanes, probably a civil air patrol unit, was based at Plum Island.

This combination of military and civilian craft, under military control, was used for reconnaissance and offshore patrol to locate German U-boats and their victims along the New England coast. The airport was also used during the war to make movies such as "Wake Island" with naval aircraft based at N.A.S. Squantum. Polando left in 1942 to fly planes for radar tests at MIT, and then to serve in the Army Air Force.

Frothingham continued to operate the airport for the next twenty-four years. In 1946, he added a second runway (the current grass strip) and built an additional hangar. Frothingham, who had the sole northeast dealership for Aeronca airplanes in the 1940s and 1950s, provided a variety of aviation services, including maintenance and flight training. The Raytheon Company used the airport for radar testing during this period.

In 1966, Richard Hordon and two partners purchased the airport operation from Frothingham. Hordon bought out his partners within a few years and operated the airport for the next thirty-four years. In 1977, a fire destroyed the earlier hangars and office building. Several months later, the Great Blizzard of 1978 caused extensive flooding that damaged the runway and the T hangars and destroyed a number of planes.

These facilities were soon replaced, and the airport continued providing aircraft maintenance, pilot training and services for transient aircraft, and served as a base for crop-dusting, aerial photography, parcel delivery, and occasional med flights. In the 1970s, airline pilot Geert Frank used the airport to restore a large number of World War II-era airplanes, and the appearance of these unique planes provided an additional attraction for plane watchers along the Plum Island Turnpike. In the 1980s, the airport became the local center for ultralight aircraft.

Grassy dunes merge the brilliant sky on Plum Island. (*Dan Graovac photo*)

From 2001 to 2006 a non-profit organization, Plum Island Community Airfield, Inc. (PICA), directed activity. Since October 2006, the airport has been leased from Historic New England. Since then, a hangar has been constructed and the museum has been improved. In July 2010, the asphalt runway was resurfaced. The parking lot is sometimes used to shuttle music fans to "porch concerts" on Plum Island.

23

A Rumrunning Boat, a Foggy Plum Island Evening and a Coast Guardsman Is Killed During Prohibition

During Prohibition (1920–1933), Plum Island was a dumping ground for gangs transporting illegal alcohol. Cases of whiskey were off-loaded from large vessels offshore, and small boats would bring in the contraband. This essay is included because it tells a dynamic story of a fatal event that took place on the island almost a century ago.

One of the key roles of the Coast Guard in recent years is patrolling U.S. and international waters to interdict vessels smuggling illegal drugs. Coast Guard cutters travel the lower Atlantic and much of the Pacific in search of drug smugglers. The Coast Guard vessels are armed and dangerous.

Today, valuable technology can help identify vessels with contraband. In southern seas, small submarine-like fast-boats have been stopped and boarded. Tons of illegal drugs have been confiscated.

During Prohibition, government vessels from Maine to Key West, Fla., were on the alert for boats carrying beer, wine and whiskey. New England states were especially plagued by rumrunners, in part because the coastal states are close to foreign ports such as those in Canada.

Here is an explanation by author Everett S. Allen, who wrote *The Black Ships, Rumrunners of Prohibition* (Boston, Toronto: Little, Brown and Co., 1965):

> The Coast Guard was frequently, often painfully, reminded of the smugglers' successes and its own complex difficulties in attempting to combat a popular traffic. Entrepreneurs had money enough to buy whoever and whatever had to be bought, principals had the sympathy of perhaps every other man on the street, and militant activists shared the government's view that the law enforcer and rumrunner were enemies and that this was war.

The following is a New England story by two Coast Guard veterans that focuses on one fatal instance of the Coast Guard battling the rumrunners years ago. It is an unfortunate tale because one Coastie was killed by friendly gunfire. It was written by David Considine, BMCS, USCG (ret.) and Mark DuPont, CWO, USCG (ret.) (2012). Their essay has appeared in *New England Coast Guard Stories* by Dyke Hendrickson (The History Press, 2020).

Here is the story: The crews at the Plum Island Coast Guard station and the crews from Base Seven in Gloucester were delegated the duty to patrol the shallow waters of Plum Island Sound and Ipswich Bay with smaller, more maneuverable vessels, while the larger picket boats remained a fair distance offshore. The Plum Island station would use its 26-foot motor surfboat on nightly patrols to cover its portion of Plum Island Sound and Ipswich Bay. Coast Guard Headquarters had received a letter on April 11, 1929, issuing instructions on how Coast Guard vessels were to identify themselves while operating in support of the rum war. This letter was read to the Plum Island crews multiple times by Herman Schwartz BMC, the officer in charge of the Plum Island station. This letter included instruction on illuminating the CG Ensign (the flag flown on all Coast Guard vessels as a means of identification) with a spotlight, and instruction on the use of warning shots and disabling fire.

Monday, Aug. 4, 1930, was a normal Monday at the Plum Island Coast Guard Station, and the daily chores, training and boat work were finished early in anticipation of the night patrol. Botswain Mate 1st Class Louis E. Pratt was the duty coxswain for the 26-foot motor surfboat. Also on duty that day was Cleo Faulkingham, a 22-year-old surfman, who had been in the Coast Guard for two years, and four months. BMC Schwartz sent Pratt and Faulkingham to "guard the entrance to the Ipswich River."

Louis Pratt was from Burlington, VT, but had moved to Kittery, Maine, when he was 16. It was here he felt the call of the sea, and decided to join the Coast Guard, enlisting at the Plum Island Coast Guard station on Dec. 16, 1922. He served at the Plum Island station and left the service a year later, having fulfilled his year-long commitment. He took two weeks off, and then re-enlisted, this time at the Portsmouth Harbor, N.H., station. Here he would stay three years until January 1927 when he was promoted to Boatswain's Mate 1st Class. Following his promotion, he was transferred back to the Plum Island station. Pratt was married to Margaret Adams Pratt, and the father of a four-year-old daughter, both of whom lived in Kittery, Maine.

On Aug. 4, Pratt and Faulkingham were issued two .45 caliber automatic pistols and ammunition. They usually would wait until 8 p.m. to depart for the patrol area, but on this night they left at 7:30 p.m. as they had been told to drop a passenger off at Ipswich Bluffs. After leaving the passenger, they proceed to Ipswich Neck Wharf, arriving a little after 8 p.m. After tying up they were approached by two men, one showing a police badge and identifying himself as Charles Mackenzie, a lieutenant from the Winthrop, (Mass.) Police Department. Mr. Mackenzie would then recount a strange tale to the two young Coast Guardsmen.

Mr. Mackenzie informed them that his boat had caught fire earlier in the day and the motor was disabled. He and his friend had anchored the boat and then towed it to shore. Mr. Mackenzie asked Pratt to go and find his vessel and tow it to Ipswich. There has been some speculation that the lieutenant may have been involved in some sort of nefarious activity, but this was never proven. The two Coast Guardsmen agreed and left the pier at about 9:15 p.m. heading out to Ipswich and heading toward Essex, where Mr. Mackenzie had told them he had anchored the boat. Little did Pratt and Faulkingham know but the disabled boat had already been discovered.

Base Seven in Gloucester was a busy Coast Guard installation in the late 1920s and 1930s, housing a surface operations unit and an aviation detachment. On Aug. 4, 1930, the commander of Base Seven, Commander E. A. Coffin, had departed on annual leave

The birthplace of the Coast Guard is Newburyport, and stories abound of adventures—and misadventures—of boaters near Plum Island.

to New London, Conn., leaving the executive officer, Chief Boatswain Oscar Vinje, in charge.

In May 1929, CDR Coffin had written to Coast Guard headquarters, outlining:

> What I thought were pertinent reasons for establishing a patrol in the Essex River, which was too shallow for our patrol and picket boats to operate in, and I requested for this duty authority to purchase an outboard boat of a certain type, and a motor for use with the boat.

The request was denied due to a lack of funding. A short while later CDR Coffin purchased a small outboard hull using money from the canteen fund. He again wrote headquarters, this time informing them of the purchase and asking for funds to procure an outboard motor for the newly acquired hull. This request was allowed, and the boat was fully outfitted by the latter part of June 1930. The outboard was 16 feet long, had a 32-horsepower outboard and was painted grey with "U.S. Coast Guard Base Seven" painted in white letters on both sides of the hull.

On July 28, CDR Coffin's plan to "lie under the bank near the mouth of the (Essex) river, perfectly dark and quiet, and wait for anything to come in," was finally put into action. For five nights, starting Monday, July 28 and continuing until Friday, Aug. 1, three Coast Guardsmen went out to the river under the command of Warrant Officer (boatswain) John J. Olsen. Chief Motor Machinist Mate Charles Palmquist and Chief Motor Machinist's Mate Hugh Olmstead were acting as crew.

These five nights were uneventful and no patrol was scheduled for Saturday, Aug. 2. Chief Palmquist took charge of the small boat on Sunday, Aug. 2, and Chief Olmstead would take the Monday night patrol. He chose as his crewman, Fireman First Class Clifford J. Hudder, who had only been in the service for 11 months. Chief Olmstead had no formal weapons training in the Coast Guard, only receiving training on the aircraft machine guns while in the Army Air Service. He had never been on a nighttime boarding or had charge of a Coast Guard small boat prior to leaving Base Seven on Monday, Aug. 4. Clifford Hudder, 21, had been less formal training and had never been trained in boarding boats. This was his first night patrol. Neither Chief Olmstead nor Fireman 1st Class Hudder had read or had been advised of the headquarters letter regarding Law Enforcement Circular of 11 April 1929.

A Fateful Day in Coast Guard History

Chief Olmstead and Hudder were issued a Lewis machine gun with two loaded pans of ammunition and one 45-caliber automatic pistol with five loaded clips. They left Base Seven between 6:30 and 7 p.m. They first stopped at Ten Pound Island off Gloucester to get a sweater for Hudder. Neither man was in uniform. Hudder was wearing dungaree pants, a sweater, a sheepskin, black shoes and no hat. Chief Olmstead's "chief" cap was the only identifying article of clothing he was wearing.

Olmstead and Hudder then headed out of the Annisquam River, and turned to port to head west to the entrance to the Essex River. Sunset on Aug. 4, 1930 was listed at 8 p.m., and darkness began to fall on Ipswich Bay. Once at the mouth of the Essex River, Hudder reported seeing a vessel along the shore near Castle Neck. Hudder would later testify that Olmstead ordered him to display the ensign on the bow of the outboard boat. Olmstead "thought (this vessel) may have something to do with rum running."

When they arrived on the scene they found a white cabin cruiser with no one aboard. Once alongside, it was evident that there was fire smoldering in the engine room, and Olmstead jumped aboard and extinguished the fire using an old coat he found onboard. He also used some soaked canvas. After looking around the boat he found "things were scattered around pretty much, the locker door was open, and it looked (to him) as though it had been left in a hurry."

Olmstead relayed his belief that this boat must be involved in rum-running, and he told Hudder they would stay there for the night and wait to see of "the rummies" returned.

Soon Hudder noticed a light off to seaward. They watched the area where he had seen the light, and soon the light flashed again. Olmstead told Hudder, "Here comes a rummy for sure." Olmstead would later recount that he told Hudder to "Jump in our outboard and pull it alongside and hand me the machine gun because I thought it was a rummy."

He instructed Hudder, "When I give the order, to turn on the lights and put the search light on the Coast Guard ensign, and to fire warning shots, and to be sure to do it because things must be carried out quickly."

The other vessel was still approaching, and when Olmstead could make out the bow, he told Hudder to put the lights on and fire the warning shots. Hudder would later testify he turned the running lights on, then trained the searchlight onto the ensign and fired seven warning shots. Hudder testified, "Almost at the same time Olmstead hollered at the other boat to come along side, that we wanted to board it." He then recounted, "A short while after this, from the other boat, I heard someone holler, 'Give it to her' or 'Give it to them.'"

Olmstead at this point, "immediately dropped behind his machine gun and opened fire about center way of this craft, thinking that there was the engine room about be aboard at this boat."

"I fired the machine gun at three different times. I just shot a few in it and waited to see if anything happened, and then shot a few more," Olmstead later recounted. He then had Hudder fire two illumination flames and saw the white vessel heading away from them. He tried to give chase to the outboard boat but the engine wouldn't start.

All in all, seven rounds were fired from the 45-caliber pistol and 29 rounds were fired from the Lewis machine gun. Twenty of the machine-gun slugs would hit the hull of the Plum Island motor surfboat.

Meanwhile, Pratt and Faulkingham had left Ipswich Neck wharf and safely navigated through the shifting shoals of the mouth of Plum Island Sound into open water. They turned to starboard once they were alongside the outer buoy and headed east toward the mouth of the Essex River. Approximately 10 minutes later Faulkingham would notice a dark object off the bow. Faulkingham turned the tiller slightly and headed the motor surfboat towards the object, thinking that must be the vessel they went looking for.

The area can seem tranquil today, but in 1930, a Coast Guardsman was killed by friendly fire near the island.

Pratt was now up by the bow with a five-cell flashlight and was trying to illuminate the object. About 85 yards off, the object they could see now was a boat. A light flashed on the boat. Faukingham would later testify, "About that time we heard a shot and in a few moments a machine gun started."

Both men dropped down in the boat. Pratt said to Faulkingham, "We had better get away." It was obvious to Faulkingham that Pratt thought it was a rumrunner shooting at them. Faulkingham threw the tiller to starboard and the motor lifeboat lumbered to port to try to evade the gunfire.

Faulkingham heard Pratt say, "I'm hit, are you?"

Fauklingham said, "Not yet."

Two flares were sent up from the area of the suspected rum boat. Faulkingham put the throttle to full and headed back in the director of Ipswich Neck Wharf. Within 45 minutes, they were at the wharf, and Faulkingham enlisted the help of some local residents to get Pratt to the Cable Memorial Hospital in Ipswich.

Surfman Faulkingham took the motor lifeboat back to the Plum Island station to report the incident to the officer in charge. Faulkingham would later testify they never heard any shouts from the disabled vessel, or heard any commands, to "come alongside." He would also testify that neither he nor Pratt had yelled "Give it to them."

Dr. O. F. Fountaine of Rowley was called at 10:30 p.m. When he arrived 10 minutes later, he recalled that Pratt was suffering from "hemorrhage and shock, he was conscious and in his right mind." Dr. Fountaine testified that Pratt told him, "he went out looking for a boat that had been adrift somewhere near Ipswich Beach." Dr. Fountaine also testified that Pratt had said, "Didn't have a chance, no warning at all, didn't have a chance."

Louis Pratt was still alive when his wife arrived at the hospital less than three hours after the shooting. He recognized his wife and asked if she had brought their daughter. Louis Pratt succumbed to his injuries shortly after, passing away in the earning morning of Aug. 5, 1930.

A Board of Inquiry found that Olmstead, chief motor machinest [*sic.*] mate, be brought to trial by the general court on charges of violating a lawful regulation issued by the Secretary of the Treasury, to wit, "No person shall be negligent or careless in obeying orders or culpably inefficient in the performance of duty."

It was recommended that Chief Boatswain Oscar Vinje be reprimanded for not informing himself while temporarily in command of Base Seven of the plans and details of the patrol on the night of Aug. 4.

Olmstead did stand court martial, but a jury rendered a verdict of not guilty, stating that the serious charges had not been proven beyond a reasonable doubt. Vinje was cleared of wrongdoing.

The study by Considine and DuPont ended by saying, "Today's world and circumstances will thrust our Guardians into a very similar circumstance that Louis Pratt faced. As former Coast Guard Commandant, Adm. Thad Allen has summarized, "All threats—All Hazards. Louis Pratt encourages us to make sure we are truly, Semper Paratus—Always Ready."

24

A Cleaner Merrimack River Will Help Plum Island

This is a story I wrote for a North Shore magazine in 2021. It suggests that keeping the river clean will greatly help Plum Island.

The Merrimack River is one of the great assets of the North Shore. But several years ago, it was named by a national advocacy organization, American Rivers, as one of the most vulnerable waterways in the country. Sometimes it appears to be getting dirtier, not cleaner.

I have written a book about this situation titled, *Merrimack: The Resilient River, An Illustrated Profile of the Most Historic River in New England*. The publication is an examination of a valuable resource that is in trouble. It is not facing disaster. Residents use kayaks, canoes, motorboats and sailboats to enjoy the Merrimack. People fish. Some swim, though they should not do so after a heavy rain. Thousands each day walk along the waterway or view it from the road. Close to a half-million people get their drinking water from it.

But the health of this historic river is too important to ignore as it once was.

The Merrimack River has numerous credentials that qualify it as the "most historic" waterway in the region.

Its creds include the following: the birthplace of the Coast Guard (Newburyport, 1790); the start of the industrial revolution (hydro-powered mills in Lowell, 1820s); the first planned industrial city (Lawrence, *circa* 1847); the discovery of a technology to produce cleaner drinking water, (Lawrence, *circa* 1890); and the site of one of the first victories in organized labor (Lawrence, 1912).

In addition to being a river of historical dimensions, it is also one of the most resilient rivers in the country. For two centuries, it was seriously polluted. Because of discharges from textile mills, its waters often turned orange or green depending on the dye being used at a given mill. Some who used it for drinking water got sick.

For many decades, a community's wastewater would be sent almost directly into the river. That would include effluent from residential toilets and industrial waste from factories. Until the early 1970s, many communities possessed only the most rudimentary of the sewage-treatment plants.

A humpback whale feeds off Plum Island in the summer of 2021. (*Dan Graovac photo*)

Considering the European discovery of the river was by Champlain in 1605 and the (Newbury) region settled in 1635, this river has a long history of surviving the manmade elements.

Check the roster:

Newburyport, building on its revitalized brick downtown and its location at the intersection of the Merrimack and Atlantic, is thriving.

Salisbury is a haven for campers and fried-dough consumers alike; Amesbury is enhancing its location on the river each year.

Haverhill, Lowell and Manchester, N.H., have made remarkable commercial and residential comebacks. Nashua and Concord, N.H., are prosperous. Lawrence, too, has launched a civic drive to improve the downtown, upgrade housing and enhance education.

Scores of smaller communities are also thriving.

Contemplating the admirable Merrimack, it is noteworthy to realize that most Americans didn't advocate for the environment until the '60s.

Rachel Carson's *Silent Spring* rang a bell in the early '60s. And the Cuyahoga River (Ohio) fire in the 1969 was an outrageous wake-up call to force political action to halt destructive polluting. The resulting Clean Water Act of 1972 kicked off a mandated, federally funded approach to cleaner water. That was about 50 years ago. Because of federal funding and supervision, the Merrimack is one American river that has been made healthier.

Still, users must be wary. In 2021, some who boat, fish and hike the Merrimack have seen effluent in the water after rainstorms. Dogs that romp in the river have acquired sores. Needles that once conveyed dangerous drugs have been found on its shores.

But recreation is not the only concern. Close to a half-million residents get their drinking water from the Merrimack. It is scientifically treated, of course, but a cleaner river would make everyone more secure.

Combined sewage overflows (CSOs) are still a problem. This occurs as a result of rainwater coming into sewage-treatment plants through municipal pipes. After large, fast-moving storms, an abundance of rainwater mixes with effluent in treatment plants. The plant can't accommodate both effluent and stormwater, so the entire amount is discharged into the river. Millions of gallons of effluent enter the Merrimack each year.

In addition to minimizing CSOs, advocates hope they can limit entry of chemicals released by some companies near the river. And they want to slow the residential and commercial development that threatens wetlands, streams, and tributaries.

As the anniversary of the Clean Water Act of 1972 reaches a half-century, the river has improved. As a result of this legislation, engineered by Sen. Edmund Muskie of Maine, the Merrimack has made a significant comeback.

Also, amendments to the Clean Water Act in 1987 may have saved rivers such as the Merrimack. In the '80s, President Ronald Reagan wanted to abolish federal grants for sewage treatment. But proponents, led by Sen. George Mitchell of Maine, were able to compromise with the president. As a result, low-interest loans were made available for construction of sewage-treatment projects.

Following the departure of the Trump Administration, federal legislators on the North Shore are seeking these low-interest federal revolving loans once again. Local elected officials developing an alert system that will notify communities downstream when CSOs have occurred upstream.

And the Merrimack River Commission was created in the past year to provide more governmental attention. Thus, more help is in the pipeline for one of the North Shore's most glittering assets.

Day is done on the Merrimack River, a body of water that residents and elected leaders alike are trying to keep clean. (*Courtesy photo*)

Bibliography

Atherton, S., numerous interviews with this Plum Island photographer and resident

Cheney, R., *Maritime History of Merrimac Shipbuilding* (Newburyport, Mass.: Newburyport Press, 1964)

Cheney, R., *The Cheney Collection* (Newburyport, Mass.: Custom House Maritime Museum, 1992)

Currier, J. J., *History of Newbury, Mass, 1635–1902* (Boston: Damrell & Upham, 1902)

DiZoglio, state Sen. D., podcast interview, *Life Along the Merrimack* methods to halt pollution (2021)

Doyle, J. F., *Life in Newburyport, 1950–1985* (Portsmouth: Peter Randall Publisher, 2010)

Eagle-Tribune, North Andover, Mass. (Archives of this newspaper were consulted regularly, 2019–2020)

Eigerman, J., city councilor, podcast interview, Newburyport, *Life Along the Merrimack* (2021)

Evans-Dale, L. and Utterbach, M. (eds.), *The ABCs of Newburyport Maritime History* (Newburyport, Mass., booklet for Custom House Maritime Museum, 2014)

Graovac, D., chair of the board of the Merrimack River Watershed Council, discussion of his extensive photo collection, (2021)

Hendrickson, D., *The Daily News* of Newburyport, numerous articles written by Hendrickson between 2011 and 2017

Hendrickson, D., *Nautical Newburyport: A History of Captains, Clipper Ships and the Coast Guard* (Charleston, S.C.: The History Press, 2017)

Hendrickson, D., *Merrimack: The Resilient River, An Illustrated Profile of the Most Historic River in New England* (Arcadia Publishing by arrangement if Fonthill Media LLC, 2021) Historic Ipswich website, hosted by a civic group that keeps a website and an archive

Hudon, P., *Lower Merrimack: The Valley and Its Peoples; An Illustrated History* (Sun Valley, Calif.: American Historical Press, 2004)

Life Along the Merrimack, a weekly podcast at which I interview historians and politicians about the coast of Massachusetts

Macone, J., outreach historian with Merrimack River Watershed Council, podcast interviews, *Life Along the Merrimack* (2019–2021)

Massachusetts Archives Digital Repository

Merrimack River Beach Alliance, meetings and minutes, 2012–2017

Moon, David, manager of Newburyport office of the Massachusetts Audubon Society, an interview about early days of Audubon Society on Plum Island (2021)

Morison, S. E., *The Maritime History of Massachusetts, 1783–1860* (Boston, reprint, Northeastern University Press, 1979)

Parker River National Wildlife Refuge, website and publications

Reardon, Sean, mayor of Newburyport, an interview about the future of Plum Island (2021)

Smith, E. Vale, *History of Newburyport; From the Earliest Settlement of the Country to the Present Time* (published by the author in 1854, printed by Damrell and Moore in Boston)

Souder, William, *On A Farther Shore: The Life and Legacy of Rachel Carson* (New York: Crown Publishers, 2012)

Tarr, Bruce, state senator, interviews during his tenure as co-chair of the Merrimack River Beach Alliance (2012–2017)

The Daily News, Newburyport (Archives of this newspaper were consulted regularly, 2019–2021)

Tontar, Charles, city councilor, interviews during his term as city councilor and mayoral candidate (2021)

U.S. Coast Guard, archives and photo collections

U.S. Department of the Interior, Fish and Wildlife Service, website and articles

Woodworth, G., Newburyport historian, podcast interview, *Life Along the Merrimack* (2021)

Wrack Line, the online newsletter of the Parker River National Wildlife Refuge (2021)

About the Author

Dyke Hendrickson is an author-journalist living in Newburyport, Mass., birthplace of the Coast Guard. *Plum Island: A Vulnerable Gem* is his seventh book.

He is currently a consultant with the Merrimack River Watershed Council. In that role, he speaks on Zoom to clubs, associations, and historical gatherings on the history of the Coast Guard and the Merrimack River. He also hosts a weekly podcast titled *Life Along the Merrimack* during which he interviews local and state officials about the health and history of the

Author Dyke Hendrickson, during his weekly podcast *Life Along the Merrimack*.

river. The half-hour show goes out live on local radio and cable-TV; it is also archived on YouTube. Some of the "general knowledge" that appears throughout the text came from those he interviews.

He lives near the sea with his wife, Vicki. She is the founder of the Newburyport Literary Festival, and the director of the Adult and Community Education Program in that community. They have two children, Leslie, of New York, and Drew, of Somerville, Mass.; a grandson, Nico; a daughter-in-law, Natalia; and a son-in-law, Andi.

He is a graduate of Franklin and Marshall College with a degree in history, and he did graduate work at the University of Maine. He has been a writer and/or editor with the *Portland Press Herald*, the *New Orleans Times-Picayune*, the *Boston Herald* and the *Boston Business Journal*. Other publications he has written for include *USA Today*, the *Boston Globe*, and *Tennis* magazine.

From 2012 to 2017, he was the city hall and waterfront reporter for *The Daily News* in Newburyport. Other books of a maritime nature he has written include the following: *Nautical Newburyport: A History of Captains, Clipper Ships and the Coast Guard* (2017), *New England Coast Guard Stories: Remarkable Mariners* (2020), and *Merrimack, The Resilient River: An Illustrated Profile of the Most Historic River in New England* (2021).